LIBYA FRACTURED: THE STRUGGLE FOR UNITY

HEARING

BEFORE THE

SUBCOMMITTEE ON
THE MIDDLE EAST AND NORTH AFRICA

OF THE

COMMITTEE ON FOREIGN AFFAIRS
HOUSE OF REPRESENTATIVES

ONE HUNDRED FIFTEENTH CONGRESS

SECOND SESSION

APRIL 18, 2018

Serial No. 115–125

Printed for the use of the Committee on Foreign Affairs

U.S. GOVERNMENT PUBLISHING OFFICE

WASHINGTON : 2018

29–815PDF

COMMITTEE ON FOREIGN AFFAIRS

EDWARD R. ROYCE, California, *Chairman*

CHRISTOPHER H. SMITH, New Jersey
ILEANA ROS-LEHTINEN, Florida
DANA ROHRABACHER, California
STEVE CHABOT, Ohio
JOE WILSON, South Carolina
MICHAEL T. McCAUL, Texas
TED POE, Texas
DARRELL E. ISSA, California
TOM MARINO, Pennsylvania
MO BROOKS, Alabama PAUL
COOK, California SCOTT
PERRY, Pennsylvania RON
DeSANTIS, Florida
MARK MEADOWS, North Carolina
TED S. YOHO, Florida
ADAM KINZINGER, Illinois
LEE M. ZELDIN, New York
DANIEL M. DONOVAN, Jr., New York
F. JAMES SENSENBRENNER, Jr.,
  Wisconsin
ANN WAGNER, Missouri
BRIAN J. MAST, Florida
FRANCIS ROONEY, Florida
BRIAN K. FITZPATRICK, Pennsylvania
THOMAS A. GARRETT, Jr., Virginia
JOHN R. CURTIS, Utah

ELIOT L. ENGEL, New York
BRAD SHERMAN, California
GREGORY W. MEEKS, New York
ALBIO SIRES, New Jersey
GERALD E. CONNOLLY, Virginia
THEODORE E. DEUTCH, Florida
KAREN BASS, California
WILLIAM R. KEATING, Massachusetts
DAVID N. CICILLINE, Rhode Island
AMI BERA, California
LOIS FRANKEL, Florida
TULSI GABBARD, Hawaii
JOAQUIN CASTRO, Texas
ROBIN L. KELLY, Illinois
BRENDAN F. BOYLE, Pennsylvania
DINA TITUS, Nevada
NORMA J. TORRES, California
BRADLEY SCOTT SCHNEIDER, Illinois
THOMAS R. SUOZZI, New York
ADRIANO ESPAILLAT, New York
TED LIEU, California

AMY PORTER, *Chief of Staff* THOMAS SHEEHY, *Staff Director*
JASON STEINBAUM, *Democratic Staff Director*

———

SUBCOMMITTEE ON THE MIDDLE EAST AND NORTH AFRICA

ILEANA ROS-LEHTINEN, Florida, *Chairman*

STEVE CHABOT, Ohio
DARRELL E. ISSA, California
RON DeSANTIS, Florida
MARK MEADOWS, North Carolina
ADAM KINZINGER, Illinois
LEE M. ZELDIN, New York
DANIEL M. DONOVAN, Jr., New York
ANN WAGNER, Missouri
BRIAN J. MAST, Florida
BRIAN K. FITZPATRICK, Pennsylvania
JOHN R. CURTIS, Utah

THEODORE E. DEUTCH, Florida
GERALD E. CONNOLLY, Virginia
DAVID N. CICILLINE, Rhode Island
LOIS FRANKEL, Florida
BRENDAN F. BOYLE, Pennsylvania
TULSI GABBARD, Hawaii
BRADLEY SCOTT SCHNEIDER, Illinois
THOMAS R. SUOZZI, New York
TED LIEU, California

CONTENTS

Page

WITNESSES

Mr. Christopher Blanchard, Specialist in Middle Eastern Affairs, Foreign Affairs, Defense, and Trade Division, Congressional Research Service 6

Frederic Wehrey, Ph.D., senior fellow, Middle East Program, Carnegie Endowment for International Peace 23

Ms. Alice Hunt Friend, senior fellow, International Security Program, Center for Strategic and International Studies 30

LETTERS, STATEMENTS, ETC., SUBMITTED FOR THE HEARING

Mr. Christopher Blanchard: Prepared statement 8

Frederic Wehrey, Ph.D.: Prepared statement 25

Ms. Alice Hunt Friend: Prepared statement 32

APPENDIX

Hearing notice 54

Hearing minutes 55

The Honorable Gerald E. Connolly, a Representative in Congress from the Commonwealth of Virginia: Prepared statement 56

LIBYA FRACTURED: THE STRUGGLE FOR UNITY

WEDNESDAY, APRIL 18, 2018

House of Representatives,
Subcommittee on the Middle East and North Africa,
Committee on Foreign Affairs,
Washington, DC.

The subcommittee met, pursuant to notice, at 2 o'clock p.m., in room 2172, Rayburn House Office Building, Hon. Ileana Ros-Lehtinen (chairman of the subcommittee) presiding.

Ms. Ros-Lehtinen. The subcommittee will come to order. After recognizing myself and my friend, the ranking member Deutch, for 5 minutes each for our opening statement, I then will recognize other members seeking recognition as well.

We will then hear from our witnesses. Without objection, the witnesses' prepared statements will be made a part of the record.

And members may have 5 days to insert statements and questions for the record, subject to the length limitation in the rules.

The Chair now recognizes herself for 5 minutes.

Nearly 7 years after Qaddafi's removal, Libya remains mired in civil conflict, political division, lawlessness, and economic crisis, with few signs of abating anytime soon. ISIS and al-Qaeda, though seriously degraded, are regrouping, and as we have seen in a series of car bombings this year, they are still very much capable of violence. Despite backing by the United Nations and its partners, the western-based Government of National Accord, or GNA, has not been able to provide security or consolidate power throughout Libya's vast territory, and it continues to clash with eastern-based House of Representatives backed by General Haftar and his Libyan National Army, or LNA.

Armed militias, some with ties to the LNA and GNA, profit off the lack of security and the rule of law, smuggling drugs, weapons and people, and migrants using Libya as a waypoint into Europe, suffer horrific treatment at the hands of smugglers, including torture, sexual abuse, and enslavement.

Adding to the chaos, a host of external actors continue to back different Libyan factions with the U.S. and the U.N. supporting the GNA; Egypt, the UAE, and Russia supporting Haftar, and Qatar and Turkey supporting the country's Islamist groups. And as we saw when three French soldiers were killed fighting ISIS alongside Haftar forces in 2016, even France has played both sides, sometimes assisting the U.S. and the GNA while at other times supporting Haftar and his factions.

All of this has made political reconciliation more remote, as both sides have dug in their heels and negotiations have stalled. The prospect of U.N.-backed elections this year, which were probably too soon anyway, also seems to have fallen by the wayside.

There are some encouraging signs, however, including better governance at the local and municipal levels and growth in the oil sector, which for now has saved Libya's economy from collapse. And it remains to be seen how Haftar's now-confirmed hospitalization in Paris will impact Libya's fractured state. If he is, indeed, incapacitated, will this be the opening that Libya needs for reconciliation or will there be more chaos as his coalition breaks apart and his backers look for a successor?

With the challenges I have laid out, as well as the competing foreign policy priorities elsewhere, it is perhaps understandable that this administration would be wary of spending political capital in Libya. The administration does so at its peril, however, as this is a problem that is not going away and is only going to get worse for the region, for Europe, and for U.S. interests, if it is not addressed.

Just last month, our U.S. commander in Africa stated that, "The instability in Libya and North Africa may be the most significant threat to the U.S. and our allies' interest on the continent."

Our partners in Tunisia and Egypt are already feeling the impact. Mali, Chad, and Sudan have been impacted. And we have seen how ISIS networks in Libya can reach into Europe with the Manchester and Berlin terror attacks in the last 2 years alone.

Libya's instability is a major problem for U.S. interests, and we need a concerted effort from this administration to make it a priority. It is past time to appoint a new U.S. Ambassador to Libya. And soon, as it is viable from a security standpoint, we need to consider reopening our Embassy in Tripoli to increase engagement on the ground. The administration should also fill the empty special envoy slot as soon as possible, so that the U.S. has another dedicated diplomat who can work with our partners and coordinate our Libya policy, whatever that may be.

More than anything, more than military aid, more than financial aid, Libya needs U.S. leadership, leadership that can corral the various countries' interfering in Libya, leverage our connections, and help push the political reconciliation process forward. I urge this administration to give Libya the attention that it deserves.

And with that, I am pleased to yield to my friend, Mr. Deutch, the ranking member.

Mr. DEUTCH. Thank you, Madam Chairman, for calling this hearing and for your continued recognition of Libya's importance.

I also would like to thank our panel of witnesses for attending and for their wealth of knowledge on these vital topics.

We have all been shaken and horrified by the images and stories coming out of Libya, including slave markets, dismal conditions of refugee camps, extrajudicial killings, torture in illegal retention facilities, and other human rights violations on a shocking scale. These are all issues that desperately need to be tackled and are all symptoms of the years without a functional government.

I am proud that this committee unanimously passed House Resolution 644 strongly condemning the slave auctions of migrants and refugees in Libya, but we acknowledge the only way to stop these evil practices is to see Libya set toward a path of lasting stability.

Despite the efforts of the United Nations, the internationally brokered Government of National Accord, based in Tripoli, has been far from successful. The rise of competing strongmen and militias, defined by their quickly changing loyalties, and the persistent vacuums allowing terror groups to grow, are preventing the country from moving toward stability.

And these factors of instability are enabling a humanitarian crisis to fester and worsen, emphasizing the need to address the root causes of Libya's plight. Unfortunately, the country's trajectory does not appear to have been altered over the previous year in any way that would suggest that conditions are improving.

Attempts to bring together warring parties have been hindered by fractured loyalties and varying goals. Libya's economy is disjointed and struggling to rise above the prevailing black market. This only serves to promote smuggling, trafficking, and other illicit activities. Libyans, who once benefitted from the country's oil reserves, lack opportunity and job prospects, with youth unemployment now over 40 percent.

Unfortunately, without functioning institutions, the government will continue to lack the ability to put basic structures in place for economic improvement. A continued fractured government and persistent security concerns will also prevent investment in the country.

The implications of Libya's unrest and instability don't only apply to its own security. Libya's neighbors are directly impacted by the lawlessness, movement in smuggled weapons and trafficked people, and a draw for terrorist groups seeking safe haven from regions with stronger rule of law.

As we have seen in Syria, Russia has attempted to expand its influence by exploiting the Libyan unrest. With little regard for human dignity and international law, Russia will not lead Libya toward stability. They only work toward furthering their own interests, likely at odds with our own national security priorities. That is why a coherent United States policy, along with the U.S.'s work with the U.N. to move Libya in the right direction, becomes even more pressing.

The U.S. has long focused on counterterrorism, pressuring Libya to combat the various extremist threats plaguing the country. This is continuously challenged by the difficulty in securing Libya's vast desert borders. Border security is further challenged, given the chaos of the Sahel and sub-Saharan Africa, the use of Libya as a transit point for ISIS and al-Qaeda's allied fighters, and the smuggling of weapons to various terror groups. As conflict persists among Libya's armed forces and militia groups, it appears less and less likely that border security will increase.

We maintain the goal of setting Libya on a course toward stability through a buildup of democratic institutions, the resiliency of which is not reliant upon personalities, but upon the framework of a functional government. U.S. engagement has been a challenge, given that U.S. Embassy personnel continue to operate out of Tunis. Nonetheless, we remain committed to democracy and governance and civil society programs.

Of course, the solution for Libya must be ultimately a Libyan solution. We must look at the specific population needs, cultural dynamics, tribal identities, and social conditions to find a path forward that works for Libyans. And despite the obvious challenges, it remains in our national security interest, and those of international stability, that we continue to encourage and assist Libya in moving toward stability and preventing dangerous transnational terror groups from finding safe haven there. Only once good, honest, and comprehensive governance takes hold will the root cause of the horrors that we have witnessed be truly addressed.

I look forward to hearing from our witnesses as to how Libya can best move forward on the path of reconciliation that resists the influence of non-state actors and provides stability and opportunity for all of the people of Libya.

And I yield back.

Ms. ROS-LEHTINEN. Thank you very much, Mr. Deutch, our ranking member.

And now, I would like to turn to the members of our subcommittee for any opening statements they would like to make, and we will start with Mr. DeSantis of Florida.

Mr. Kinzinger of Illinois?

Mr. KINZINGER. Thank you, Madam Chair.

I don't have a lot to say, except that, obviously, we find ourselves in a pretty tough situation there, a lot of debate, a lot of questions, but I think it is obvious that, with the part of the world that Libya is in, and potentially the ramifications for the rest of the world, including Europe, of a failed Libyan state, it is important that we stayed engaged.

Unfortunately, we have been seeing Libya sometimes how we have been seeing, for instance, Syria, which is just through the lens of a counter-ISIS campaign, which is important, but this is a much bigger issue than just a fight against terror.

So, I appreciate all of you being here, and I want to thank the chair for having this hearing.

And I will yield back.

Ms. ROS-LEHTINEN. Thank you very much, Adam.

Mr. Chabot of Ohio?

Mr. CHABOT. Thank you, Madam Chair. Thank you for holding this important hearing, and I will be very brief.

I happened to be the chair of this committee when Qaddafi fell, when the so-called Arab Spring was happening, et cetera.

Ms. ROS-LEHTINEN. You might have been the cause of all these democracy movements.

Mr. CHABOT. Yes, maybe. Maybe. All this democracy.

But I was in Libya with the Ambassador a month before he and three other brave Americans were killed. And so, it was obviously a traumatic experience for our country. It is one of the, I think, most unfortunate circumstances, not that incident necessarily, but just the overall chaos that ensued after the fall and where we are now. There is a tremendous amount that needs to be done in Libya.

Hopefully, this hearing will shed some light on that. And so, I thank you very much for holding it. Thank you.

Ms. ROS-LEHTINEN. Thank you very much. That was such a tragedy. Thank you so much, Mr. Chabot.

Mr. Cicilline of Rhode Island is recognized.

Mr. CICILLINE. Thank you, Madam Chairman, and the ranking member, for holding this hearing.

Libya has been a difficult challenge for the United States and our allies since the fall of Muammar al-Qaddafi. As we have seen in many other places, it is far easier to topple a government than to rebuild a new one. Libya continues to be challenged by political fragmentation, rival factions, decentralization, terrorist threats, and the challenges of migration.

I want to take a moment in my opening to recognize and remember the men who were killed in the attack on our consulate in Libya in 2002. Ambassador Chris Stevens, Sean Smith, Glen Doherty, and Tyrone Woods served our country with honor and gave their lives in defense of our freedoms.

I thank our witnesses for appearing here today and look forward to hearing your perspectives on what we can do to help stabilize Libya and ensure a viable path forward, so the people of Libya can live in peace.

Thank you. And with that, I yield back.

Ms. ROS-LEHTINEN. Thank you so much, Mr. Cicilline.

Seeing no other requests for time, I am so pleased to recognize our witnesses.

First, we are delighted to welcome Mr. Christopher Blanchard, a specialist in Middle Eastern Affairs at the Congressional Research Service. Mr. Blanchard has covered developments in Libya since 2005 and served as an election observer for Libya's first post-Qaddafi elections in 2012, very historic.

Thank you for being here today. We appreciate all the work you have done over the years at CRS, and we look forward to your testimony, Mr. Blanchard.

Next, we are delighted to welcome Dr. Frederic Wehrey. Did I do that right? Thank you. He is senior fellow in the Middle East Program at Carnegie Endowment for International Peace and a 21-year veteran of the U.S. Air Force.

Thank you for your service, Dr. Wehrey.

He has just had a book published about Libya, and has written many articles on Libya and the wider Middle East.

Thank you for your service again, and thank you for your testimony today, Doctor.

And finally, we are delighted to welcome Ms. Alice Friend. Is that right? Just like that? Okay. Friend, that is a great name.

She is senior fellow in the International Security Program at the Center for Strategic and International Studies. Previously, Ms. Friend served in various roles at the Department of Defense, including as Principal Director for African Affairs in the Office of the Under Secretary of Defense for Policy. She has also held numerous research positions at CSIS and at the Center for New American Security.

Thank you for being here today, and we also look forward to your testimony.

As I had said previously, your written testimony will be made a part of the record. Please feel free to summarize.

We will start with you, Mr. Blanchard.

STATEMENT OF MR. CHRISTOPHER BLANCHARD, SPECIALIST IN MIDDLE EASTERN AFFAIRS, FOREIGN AFFAIRS, DEFENSE, AND TRADE DIVISION, CONGRESSIONAL RESEARCH SERVICE

Mr. BLANCHARD. Thank you Chairman Ros-Lehtinen, Ranking Member Deutch, members of the committee, for inviting me to testify today on behalf of the Congressional Research Service on Libya. I will summarize my testimony by briefly making three observations.

First, as you have discussed, several internal and external factors are disrupting Libya's post-Qaddafi transition. These factors are interrelated and they have been difficult to overcome. For example, transitional leaders and institutions with competing claims to legitimacy have accumulated in Libya since 2011. This challenges U.S. preferences to work with and through a single national government partner.

Since December 2015, the U.N. Security Council and the United States have recognized the negotiated GNA as Libya's governing authority. This seeks to confer international legitimacy on the GNA and to encourage unification. But, nevertheless, the GNA and its eastern-Libya-based rivals have made little progress, as you have noted. The GNA's reach remains limited and, importantly, it relies on militias for security support.

In 2017, U.N. officials launched an action plan to move the transition promptly and to renew the legitimacy of these Libyan institutions, but its implementation has faltered. Meanwhile, the power of armed non-state groups remains unmatched, and there is a lawless atmosphere that persists. Militias, criminals, and terrorists, including remnants of the Islamic State, operate with impunity in some areas, endangering civilians and committing human rights abuses. These entities exploit instability and state weakness for political and financial gain. This creates powerful incentives for them to maintain the unstable status quo. Thousands of migrants, refugees, and internally displaced persons remain particularly vulnerable.

Many foreign governments are seeking to mitigate transnational threats emanating from Libya, and some are actively working to shape the transition's outcome in line with their preferences. Libya's oil resources, its geographic location, and weak institutions all raise the stakes of its instability for others. Libyan-based terrorists, traffickers, and armed groups pose risks to U.S. partners in North Africa, the Sahel, Europe, and beyond. Locally organized Libyan actors cooperate and compete amongst themselves and with these outsiders. Egypt, the United Arab Emirates, and the European states are all engaging directly with different Libyan factions for a range of specific purposes.

As my written testimony and reporting for CRS describe in more detail, this produces a complex and opaque web of overlapping interests and rivalries. Taken together, these challenges and dynamics are likely to last and to have enduring effects, even if the current mediation efforts improve.

Second, U.S. policy in Libya has two main goals. It seeks to eliminate Libya-based terrorists and combat other transnational threats, and it seeks to support the transition to a unified, inclusive, and accountable government as the basis for long-term stability. The Trump and Obama administrations have used different blends of diplomacy and military operations, sanctions, and foreign aid to achieve relatively consistent objectives over time. Diplomatically, the United States is lending support to U.N. mediation rather than seeking to engineer a U.S.-defined solution. Given that zero-sum attitudes have divided post-Qaddafi Libya, U.S. policymakers judge that an inclusive, Libyan-defined solution is more likely to result in stability than solutions imposed by force or by outsiders. Current policy also reflects the judgment that a settlement can't be reached without international support and coordination.

So, what more can the United States do to support Libya's transition? Events since 2011 suggest a series of factors to consider. More active U.S. diplomacy and more robust assistance could boost actors that share U.S. goals, but also could create enduring costs for the United States, link the United States to actors that lack domestic legitimacy, or invite others to intervene similarly. Less active U.S. involvement could reduce diplomatic and financial burdens on the Unites States and could simplify relations with outsiders, but it might also result in less desirable security outcomes. If security were to deteriorate rapidly, containment costs could increase, pressure on U.S. partners could rise, and calls for new U.S. intervention could emerge.

Third, for Congress, different scenarios may raise unique questions, but certain topics have been shown to have lasting relevance in Libya, regardless of how conditions have evolved. These include the balance of U.S. diplomatic, military, and foreign aid efforts; the roles of other outside actors; frameworks defined by the U.N. Security Council; funding and terms for U.S. assistance; the selection and vetting of U.S. partners, and authorizations for the use of military force.

This concludes my brief remarks. Thank you for the opportunity to testify, and I look forward to your questions.

[The prepared statement of Mr. Blanchard follows:]

Congressional Research Service
Informing the legislative debate since 1914

Statement of

Christopher M. Blanchard
Specialist in Middle Eastern Affairs

Before

Committee on Foreign Affairs
Subcommittee on Middle East and North Africa
U.S. House of Representatives

Hearing on

"Fractured Libya: The Struggle for Unity"

April 16, 2018

Congressional Research Service
7-5700
www.crs.gov
<Product Code>

Thank you Chairman Ros-Lehtinen, Ranking Member Deutch, and Members of the committee, for inviting me to testify on behalf of the Congressional Research Service on Libya.

Overview

Libya's political transition has been disrupted by armed non-state groups and threatened by the indecision and infighting of interim leaders. After an armed uprising ended the 40-plus-year rule of Muammar al Qadhafi in late 2011, interim authorities proved unable to form a stable government, address pressing security issues, reshape the country's public finances, or reconcile. Qadhafi left state institutions weak and deprived Libyans of experience in self-government, compounding stabilization challenges.

Elections for legislative bodies and a constitutional drafting assembly held in 2012 and 2014 were administered transparently, but were marred by declining rates of participation, threats to candidates and voters, and zero-sum political competition. Insecurity became prevalent in Libya following the 2011 conflict and deepened in 2014, driven by overlapping ideological, personal, financial, and transnational rivalries. Issues of dispute have included governance, military command, national finances, and control of oil infrastructure.

At present, armed militia groups and locally organized political leaders remain the most powerful arbiters of public affairs. An atmosphere of persistent lawlessness has enabled militias, criminals, and Islamist terrorist groups to operate with impunity, further endangering civilians' rights and safety. The United Nations (U.N.) Security Council and the United States have recognized a Government of National Accord (GNA). Based in the capital, Tripoli, it has made little progress in overcoming disputes that have split the country politically and geographically since 2014. A rival governing entity is based in eastern Libya. Meanwhile, Libya's remote south suffers from neglect and remains both an arena for domestic conflicts and a permissive transit zone for migrants, criminals, traffickers, and terrorist groups. U.S. Africa Command (AFRICOM) has emphasized the importance of a political solution for stability, and in March 2018, told Congress that, in light of prevailing turmoil, "the risk of a full-scale civil war remains real."

U.S. officials and other international actors have worked since 2014 to convince Libyan factions and their various external supporters that inclusive, representative government and negotiation are preferable to competing attempts to achieve dominance through force of arms. The U.N. Security Council has authorized financial and travel sanctions on individuals and entities responsible for threatening "the peace, stability or security of Libya," obstructing or undermining "the successful completion of its political transition," or supporting others who do so. A U.N. arms embargo is in place, and U.S. executive orders provide for sanctions against individuals undermining Libya's transition.

In December 2015, some Libyan leaders endorsed the U.N.-brokered political agreement to create the Government of National Accord to oversee the completion of the transition. GNA Prime Minister-designate Fayez al Sarraj and members of a GNA Presidency Council have attempted to implement the agreement and have competed for influence with political figures and armed forces based in eastern Libya, including Field Marshal Khalifa Haftar's "Libyan National Army" (LNA) movement. A U.N.-sponsored Action Plan launched in 2017 seeks to complete Libya's transition during the coming year, and Libyans and outsiders are debating terms for its implementation. Previous mediation efforts struggled to gain traction, and outsiders have at times pursued their own agendas through ties with Libyan factions. Such competition by proxy may raise the stakes of Libya's internal rivalries and complicate negotiations.

The State Department suspended operations at the U.S. Embassy in Tripoli in July 2014 and has delayed the reintroduction of U.S. personnel on a permanent basis in light of prevailing security conditions. U.S. diplomats engage with Libyans and monitor U.S. programs in Libya via the Libya External Office (LEO) at the U.S. Embassy in Tunisia. U.S. military strikes and advice supported some Libyan forces in Operation Odyssey Lightning, a 2016 campaign to expel thousands of Islamic State (IS, aka ISIS/ISIL) supporters from the central coastal city of Sirte (**Table 1**). Periodic U.S. strikes target IS members and other terrorists. U.S. officials judge that the threats posed by IS members and Al Qaeda have been degraded, but note that these groups could resurge if overall political and security conditions deteriorate.

Table 1. Libya Map and Facts

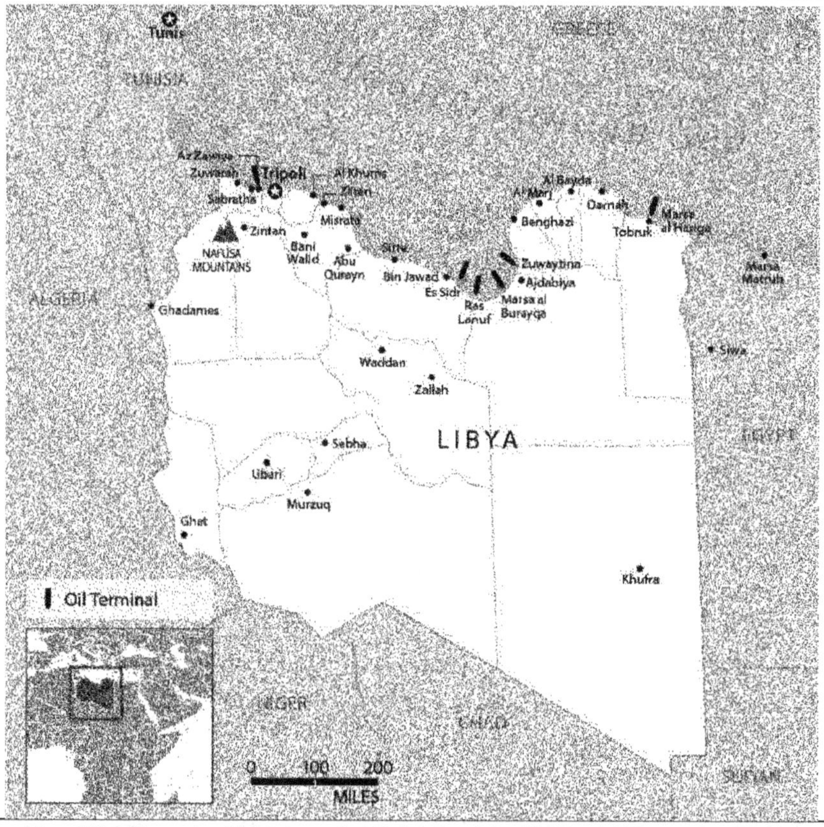

Land *Area:* 1.76 million sq. km. (slightly larger than Alaska); *Boundaries:* 4,348 km (~40% more than U.S.-Mexico border); *Coastline:* 1,770 km (more than 30% longer than California coast)

Population: 6,653,210 (July 2017 est., in 2015 the U.N. estimated 12% were immigrants), 42.9% <25 years old

GDP *PPP:* $63.14 billion; *annual real % change:* 55.1% (2017 est.); *per capita:* $9,800 (2017 est.)

Budget (spending; balance): $22.32 billion, deficit 18% of GDP (2017 est.)

External Debt: $2.927 billion (December 2017 est.)

Foreign Exchange Reserves: $69.35 billion (December 2017 est.), $124 billion (2012 est.)

Oil and natural gas reserves: 48.36 billion barrels (2017 est.); 1.505 trillion cubic meters (2017 est.)

Source: Congressional Research Service using data from U.S. State Department, Esri, United Nations, and Google Maps. Country data from CIA World Factbook, April 2018.

Congress has conditionally appropriated funding for limited U.S. transition support and security assistance programs for Libya since 2011 and is considering the Trump Administration's request for additional assistance funds for FY2019. Congress continues to shape U.S. policy toward Libya through its oversight of existing diplomatic, foreign assistance, and defense activities and its consideration of new proposals and requests. Relative resource investment and a lack of physical presence in Libya arguably limit U.S. influence on the ground.

The Administration and some Members of Congress are considering options for future engagement in Libya with two interrelated goals: supporting the emergence of a unified, capable national government, and reducing transnational threats posed by terrorists and other actors who have exploited Libya's instability. Pursuing these objectives simultaneously presents U.S. policymakers with complicated choices about relative priorities and the interrelated consequences of a range of options. Points of active discussion concern

- the nature and extent of U.S. partnership with different Libyans;
- the type, timing, and extent of U.S. assistance;
- the potential utility or costs of sanctions or other coercive measures; and
- the degree of cooperation or confrontation with other outside actors seeking to influence developments.

These issues will likely shape U.S. policy debates about Libya for the foreseeable future.

Background and Current Political Dynamics[1]

A Succession of Transitional Governments

According to Ghassan Salamé, the Special Representative of the U.N. Secretary-General (SRSG) and head of the U.N. Support Mission in Libya (UNSMIL), Libyans are struggling to overcome a political "discourse of hatred" and "mutual exclusion" that has prevented the completion of the country's transition to date.[2] This discourse is in part a legacy of Muammar al Qadhafi's decades of divisive rule and in part a product of the internal divisions, rampant insecurity, and zero sum competition that has followed Qadhafi's downfall.

Since 2011, a series of transitional governing arrangements (**Figure 1**) have been endorsed in two national elections and a constitutional drafting assembly referendum, but rates of participation have declined over time. The net result has been a de facto accrual of transitional leaders with competing claims of legitimacy, who have been locked in an inconclusive political struggle. Sustained national civil war has been avoided, but violent clashes have occurred in many areas, and the threat of wider conflict persists.

The most serious outbreak of fighting between rival Libyan groups occurred in 2014, and ultimately was defused through U.N.-backed talks. In December 2015, these negotiations led to an agreement in Skhirat, Morocco among leading factions to establish a Government of National Accord (GNA) to oversee the completion of the transition period that began after Qadhafi's fall. Rivals in eastern and western Libya nominally committed to the agreement, but in practice struggled to preserve their interests and gain advantage throughout its two-year implementation period.

---

[1] For background, see CRS Report RL33142, *Libya: Transition and U.S. Policy*, by Christopher M. Blanchard.

[2] Remarks of SRSG Ghassan Salamé to the United Nations Security Council, March 21, 2018. The U.N. Security Council created UNSMIL as an integrated special political mission in September 2011 (Resolution 2009) "at the request of the Libyan authorities to support the country's new transitional authorities in their post-conflict efforts." See [https://unsmil.unmissions.org/mandate].

In western Libya, GNA Prime Minister Fayez al Sarraj and GNA cabinet members gained administrative control over ministries and agencies in Tripoli, but did not fully consolidate their political position or establish national security control. The GNA's presence in Tripoli has been secured by the support of aligned non-state militias. Some former members of the General National Congress legislature (GNC, elected in 2012) were incorporated into a High Council of State (HCS), which was formed as an advisory and consultative body under the 2015 Skhirat agreement (also referred to as the Libyan Political Agreement, LPA).

The leaders of the eastern Libya-based House of Representatives legislature (HOR, elected in 2014) signed the 2015 Skhirat agreement, but they have prevented the HOR from fully endorsing the agreement and the GNA cabinet, challenging the GNA's claim to national authority. HOR leaders instead have supported an eastern Libya-based interim government while partnering with former Qadhafi-era military officer Khalifa Haftar and his "Libyan National Army" (LNA) coalition of military units, militia groups, and local fighters. LNA forces declared victory over numerous opposing militia groups in Benghazi last year after a costly, destructive three year battle, but the LNA does not appear capable of a military victory against rivals in western Libya in spite of threats to launch operations. Forces aligned with the GNA and the LNA have clashed in areas of central and southern Libya since mid-2017, even as some of their respective commanders and civilian officials have engaged in unity talks sponsored by Egypt.

Figure 1. Libya's Contested Transition

(Select Actors and Developments, 2011-2018)

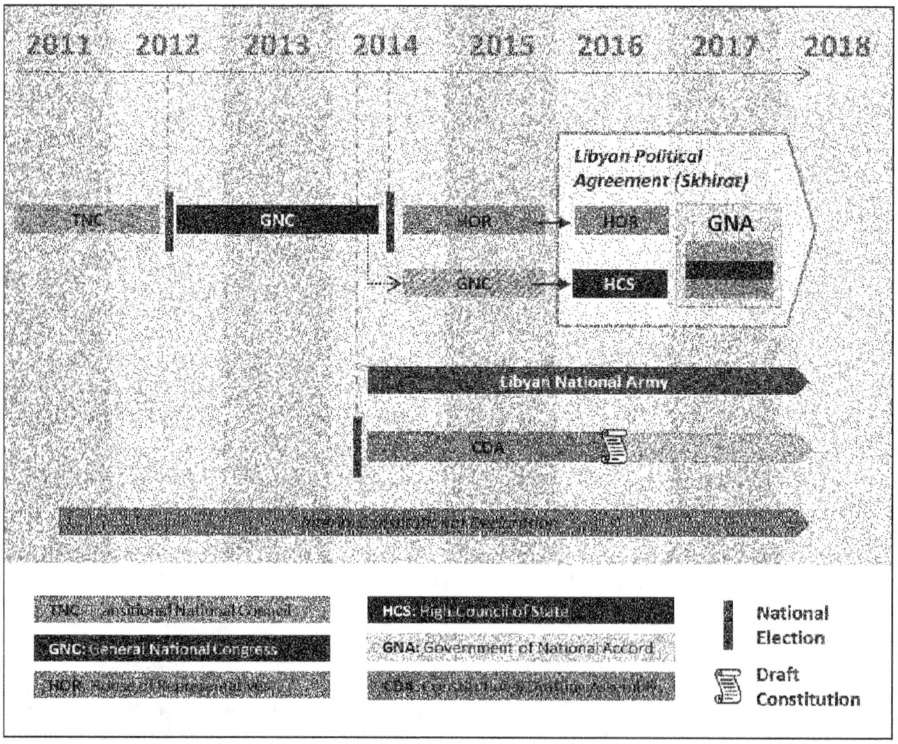

Source: Congressional Research Service.

The United Nations Action Plan

The U.N. Security Council has recognized the GNA as Libya's governing authority since 2015, in an effort to confer international legitimacy on its leaders and encourage unification efforts. When the Skhirat agreement reached the end of its originally intended duration in December 2017, the Security Council restated its endorsement of the agreement and of the GNA as enduring reference points for the completion of Libya's transition to a hoped-for permanent representative government structure. UNSMIL in September 2017 proposed an 'Action Plan for Libya' to bring the transition period to an end through a series of planned democratic exercises, including a constitutional referendum and the election of legislative and executive bodies. SRSG Salamé has stated his hope that new elections could help overcome what he views as the "shallow legitimacy" and "tenuous mandates" of present governing arrangements.[3]

The Action Plan initially focused on the negotiation of amendments to the 2015 Skhirat agreement to address issues that have prevented its implementation. These issues include differences over the size and role of the GNA's Presidency Council, the assignment of executive authority, and who holds the power to approve the leadership of national security bodies and civil service institutions. As of April 2018, the parties have not agreed to proposed amendments, and SRSG Salamé has expressed doubt that consensus on changes to the Skhirat agreement will emerge.[4] In parallel, the HOR and HCS have begun drafting and debating laws for a constitutional referendum and elections, which, if held, could obviate the need for amendments to current arrangements by granting a mandate to a new executive authority.

UNSMIL is facilitating discussions among Libyan parties and their international backers on these issues and also has begun consultations with local actors to inform and build support for a National Dialogue conference planned for later this year. According to SRSG Salamé, some Libyan municipalities are expected to proceed with local elections over the next few months. SRSG Salamé cites unspecified polling suggesting that Libyans want to hold national legislative elections.[5] He is seeking advance public commitments from rival factions that they will participate and not interfere with the conduct of such elections and that they will accept and abide by the outcome.

Recent Developments and Prospects

The U.N. Action Plan's original goal for implementation by the end of 2018 added renewed urgency to efforts to resolve Libya's political crises, but observers and officials have yet to identify any significant breakthroughs. The potential prize of a renewed electoral mandate has proven attractive to leading actors on all sides, but zero sum political calculations have thus far outweighed efforts to find common ground and move ahead. A successful national voter registration drive and leaders' continued engagement in discussions with UNSMIL are positive signs,[6] but rivals also appear to be leveraging the non-implementation of legislative and bureaucratic arrangements to influence the scope and pace of progress. Specifically, significant decisions regarding electoral legislation and timing have yet to be taken.

---

[3] Remarks of SRSG Salamé before the U.N. Security Council, March 21, 2018.

[4] SRSG Salamé told the U.N. Security Council in March 2018 that the amendments "have little chance of being passed." He also said, "The Action Plan does not depend on these amendments, and certainly, the closer Libya is to elections, the less relevant these provisional amendments become." Ibid.

[5] Address of SRSG for Libya Ghassan Salamé at the Meeting of Arab Foreign Ministers in Riyadh, Saudi Arabia, April 12, 2018.

[6] Libya's High National Election Commission (HNEC) chairman Emad Sayeh has moved forward with preparations for national elections with international technical assistance. HNEC registered one million new voters from December 2017 to March 2018, bringing the registered voter total to more than 2.4 million, roughly 53% of the eligible voter population. Abdulkader Assad, "HNEC: Number of registered voters give credibility to any elections," *Libya Observer*, April 9, 2018.

The atmosphere at the end of 2017 was particularly confrontational, as the Skhirat agreement neared its two-year anniversary and LNA leader Khalifa Haftar asserted his view that the agreement and the legitimacy of associated institutions had expired. Observers then speculated that Haftar and his supporters might resort to unilateral measures and/or seek to impose a solution by force. That outcome was avoided, but Haftar has paired subsequent statements about wanting elections "as soon as possible" with statements questioning Libya's readiness for democracy and implying that the LNA could resort to other means.[7]

In April 2018, press reports concerning Haftar's alleged incapacitation or death—reportedly due to a stroke—caused confusion and uncertainty. Analysts and observers are emphasizing the LNA coalition's potentially fractious internal makeup, speculating about its durability, and discussing the potential related implications for Libya's stability. The U.S. government has engaged Haftar and his LNA and HOR partners to encourage them to support the U.N. Action Plan, and U.S. engagement with leaders in eastern Libya in support of unity and reconciliation efforts would presumably continue in the event of lasting leadership change in the LNA or among its political partners.

In March, members of the High Council of State voted to replace Abderrahman al Swehli, a powerful western Libyan figure from Misrata and prominent critic of the LNA and HOR, with Khalid al Meshri of the Justice and Construction movement, Libya's Muslim Brotherhood-affiliated party. Al Meshri and HOR leaders have agreed to meet, and their discussions may lead to progress on required legislation for planned elections. LNA officers and GNA-affiliated military officers also have met for several rounds of talks in Cairo as part of an Egyptian government-led process that seeks to unify and reorganize Libya's national military forces.

Global concern about the trafficking and detention of migrants in western Libya has been accompanied by increased international attention to the region's political economy and security in recent months. The GNA's presence in Tripoli is underwritten by the support of powerful local militia groups, some of whom are reportedly involved in human rights abuses, crime, and illegal detentions (see below).

The Roles and Concerns of External Actors in Libya

The United States is one external actor among several seeking to influence Libya's political and security trajectory. Libya's immediate neighbors have been most directly affected by the unrest and persistent insecurity in the country. Foreign fighters from Tunisia, Algeria, Egypt, Niger, Chad, and Sudan have travelled to Libya to support various armed groups over time, and Libya-based extremists and criminal organizations have created security challenges and/or been linked to attacks in several of these countries since 2011. As noted above, Egypt is engaged in mediation efforts with Libyan military figures, leveraging its close ties to eastern Libya-based leaders and the LNA.

Across the Mediterranean, European countries share concerns about the transit of migrants from Libya and the presence in Libya of terrorist groups. The European Union has extended its efforts to respond to migrant transit at sea and initiated new efforts to train Libyan coast guard personnel and support Libyan communities that host migrants. France acknowledged conducting military operations in Libya in 2016 after three of its special forces personnel were killed there. Italy, which first deployed to Libya in 2016 to support and protect a military hospital in Misrata, approved an increase in its troop deployment in January 2018, with 400 personnel authorized for non-combat missions. Italy also has engaged with western Libyan militias to limit trafficker-supported migrant departures by sea. Jordan and the Arab Gulf States maintain links to different Libyan factions, with the United Arab Emirates having built particularly close ties with LNA leaders and others in eastern Libya.

Russia had close ties to the Qadhafi government and has been more active in cultivating relationships with Libyan actors since 2014. Russian officials portray their efforts as even handed and open to all sides in Libya, but their ties with Haftar and the LNA appear to be more robust. These ties may serve a range of purposes, including addressing Russian counterterrorism concerns, restoring Russian military ties to Libya, and balancing Western European and U.S. influence. U.S. military officials expressed concern in 2017 that Russian support for the LNA could expand in violation of the U.N. arms embargo adopted in Security Council Resolution 1970 (2011), which restricts unauthorized arms transfers to any Libyan party and from Libya.

---

[7] "Libyan Army Commander Haftar Says Libya Not Yet Mature for Democracy," *Jeune Afrique* (Paris), January 7, 2018.

Representatives of the GNA, LNA, and other armed groups have traveled to Moscow and engaged with Russian officials. The U.N. Panel of Experts established pursuant to Resolution 1973 (2011) issued a report in June 2017, documenting actual and potential violations of the Libya arms embargo and warning that foreign support to armed groups in Libya was contributing to escalation.[8] The Panel of Experts mandate was most recently extended to November 15, 2018 in Resolution 2362.

Energy Resources, Fiscal Considerations, and the Economy

Conflict and instability in Libya have taken a severe toll on the country's economy and weakened its fiscal and reserve positions since 2011. As of 2014 estimates, Libya held the largest proven crude oil reserves in Africa and the ninth largest globally. Oil and natural gas supply 97% of the government's fiscal revenue, and a combination of supply disruptions and market forces caused oil production to plummet and devastated national finances from 2014 through 2016.[9] Although state revenue has declined from its post-2011 high points, state financial obligations have increased, with public spending on salaries, imports, and subsidies all having expanded.[10] Libyan officials have identified more than 1.75 million state employees (equivalent to more than 25% of the population) and estimate that salaries consume nearly 60% of the state budget.[11] Government payments to civilians and militia members have continued since the outbreak of conflict in 2014, and Central Bank authorities have simultaneously paid salaries for military and militia forces aligned with opposing sides in the internal conflicts.

To manage deficits and continue payments of salaries and subsidies, Libyan officials have drawn on state financial reserves, but reports of delays in salary payments persist. World Bank/International Monetary Fund statistics and U.N. estimates suggest that foreign exchange reserves have fallen from their high point of $124 billion in 2012 to an estimated $69 billion in 2017.[12] In August 2017, the U.N. Secretary-General reported that the budget deficit was then "much higher than previously projected" and predicted that foreign currency reserves would remain dangerously low through the end of 2017.[13]

An expansion of oil production since mid-2017 has provided a much-needed injection of new financial resources, with domestic production remaining near 1 million bpd for most of the period from December 2017 through early April 2018. As Libyan production has rebounded, Libya has faced calls from fellow OPEC members to participate in the group's production cut agreement. Libyan authorities reportedly have agreed to recognize a cap near the current 1 million bpd level of production.[14] Fighting near the oil crescent region and intermittent shutdowns of pipelines by militias, terrorist attacks, and labor and property disputes have demonstrated the prospect of potential disruptions or production declines.

---

[8] Final report of the Panel of Experts on Libya established pursuant to resolution 1973 (2011), U.N. document S/2017/466.

[9] The estimated budget deficit was 49% of GDP in 2015 and was even greater in 2016, as "budget revenues and exports proceeds reached the lowest amounts on record because of low oil production and prices." (See World Bank, Libya's Economic Outlook–April 2017.) As of August 2016, conflict and budget shortfalls had caused oil production to plummet to below 300,000 barrels per day (bpd) out of an overall capacity of 1.6 million bpd. See, International Monetary Fund, "Arab Countries in Transition: Economic Outlook and Key Challenges" October 9, 2014; and, Sudarsan Raghavan "As oil output falls, Libya is on the verge of economic collapse," *Washington Post*, April 16, 2016.

[10] Salaries and subsidies reportedly consumed 93% of the state budget as of September 2016. Statement of SRSG Martin Kobler to the United Nations Security Council, September 13, 2016.

[11] Sami Zaptia, "Serraj spokesperson promises 2018 budget details will be revealed next week," *Libya Herald*, April 9, 2018.

[12] World Bank, Middle East and North Africa Economic Monitor, Economic and Social Inclusion to Prevent Violent Extremism, October 2016; IMF statistics cited in Missy Ryan, "Oil-rich Libya, torn by conflict, may be going broke," *Washington Post*, February 18, 2015, and UNSMIL reports, August 2017.

[13] U.N. Document, S/2017/726, Report of the Secretary-General on the United Nations Support Mission in Libya, August 22, 2017.

[14] Salma El Wardany, "Libya's Oil Output Revival Thwarted by Pipeline Explosion," Bloomberg, December 26, 2017.

In March 2018, SRSG Salamé told the U.N. Security Council that, "Libya's finances remain precarious. Despite the country now producing well over 1 million barrels a day and generating rosy macro-economic indicators, the country does not enjoy a true economic recovery."[15] Salamé warned of "signs of a looming monetary and fiscal crisis" and cautioned against "underinvestment or sabotage" of oil revenues. He also said that, "government expenditure is bloated and continues to increase, but more spending, so far, does not lead to better services."

Libyan implementing and auditing agencies have attempted to improve budget execution, but serious challenges remain. Among these challenges have been rivalries among parallel leaders of key national institutions such as the Central Bank, National Oil Company (NOC), and Libya's sovereign wealth fund—the Libya Investment Authority (LIA). These opaque, consequential rivalries have reflected the country's underlying political competition over time.

Crime, Human Rights, and Trafficking in Persons

Average Libyans have faced tenuous economic circumstances for much of the post-2011 period amid unreliable state salary and subsidy support, weak state service provision and law enforcement, inflationary pressures, and hard currency shortages. Authorities in neighboring Tunisia assert that as many as 1 million Libyans have moved there at some point since 2011. Economic hardship has amplified the negative effects of deteriorations in local security and an overall decline in respect for the rule of law. In March 2018, SRSG Salamé told the U.N. Security Council that "Libyan men, women and children are increasingly kidnapped for profit," and decried what he described as "an economic system of predation" and "plundering." In subsequent press interviews he has urged Libyan authorities and international supporters to act against prominent organized groups involved in the smuggling of people, fuel, subsidized goods, and drugs and to use investigations and sanctions to bring an end to the "predation of public money."[16]

Prominent armed groups, including the LNA and militias aligned with the GNA, reportedly are linked to a wide variety of illicit activities and maintain informal detention centers where human rights abuses take place. According to a report recently released jointly by the U.N. Office of the High Commissioner for Human Rights and UNSMIL, "Men, women and children across Libya are arbitrarily detained or unlawfully deprived of their liberty based on their tribal or family links and perceived political affiliations. Victims have little or no recourse to judicial remedy or reparations, while members of armed groups enjoy total impunity."[17]

Migrants drawn to Libya in the hope of employment or onward passage face similar threats, and, in February 2018, the U.N. Secretary-General reported to the Security Council that "Refugees and migrants continued to be subjected to violence, forced labor, and other grave violations and abuses." In 2017, the International Organization for Migration (IOM) relayed reports concerning the abuse of migrants transiting Libya and of "slave markets" operating intermittently in the country, echoing details in press accounts.[18]

---

[15] Remarks of SRSG Ghassan Salamé to the United Nations Security Council, March 21, 2018.

[16] Aidan Lewis, "Libya won't stabilise unless shadow economy smashed – U.N. envoy," Reuters, March 29, 2018.

[17] See Office of the United Nations High Commissioner for Human Rights in cooperation with the United Nations Support Mission in Libya, "Abuse Behind Bars: Arbitrary and unlawful detention in Libya," April 2018; and, Tim Eaton, "Libya's War Economy: Predation, Profiteering and State Weakness," Chatham House, April 2018.

[18] IOM, IOM Learns of 'Slave Market' Conditions Endangering Migrants in North Africa, April 11, 2017; and CNN, "People for Sale: Exposing Migrant Slave Auctions in Libya," November 2017.

International actors and the GNA have taken a series of responsive measures since late 2017, with some migrants repatriated to their countries of origin with U.N. support.[19] IOM reported in February 2018 that more than 704,000 migrants were in Libya, among more than 165,000 internally displaced persons and more than 48,400 refugees and asylum seekers from other countries identified by the United Nations High Commissioner for Refugees (UNHCR).

The IOM reported that arrivals of migrants by sea to Italy decreased 34% in 2017 compared to 2016, as arrivals declined precipitously following the implementation of an agreement between the Italian government and some west Libya-based armed groups to target traffickers and limit departures. Deaths at sea also declined in the central Mediterranean in 2017, reflecting new arrangements and intensified rescue-at-sea efforts. As of February 2018, 27 EU member states supported the European Union's EUNAVFOR MED naval mission, and the mission reported that it had saved more than 42,000 lives at sea since its inception in June 2015.[20]

U.S. Policy

Terrorist organizations active in Libya and the continuing weakness of Libya's national security bodies and government institutions pose a dual risk to U.S. and international security. Whereas U.S. intervention in Libya in 2011 was motivated largely by concern regarding threats posed to Libyans by the Qadhafi government, U.S. policy since has been defined by efforts to contain and mitigate the negative effects of state collapse and support transition efforts. Operations by Libyan partner forces, backed by U.S. military strikes, succeeded in ending the Islamic State organization's control over territory in central and western Libya during 2016, but little parallel progress has been made toward achieving durable political reconciliation.

Today, U.S. and Libyan officials in the country's various governing entities share concerns about remaining extremists, the weakness of state institutions, and flows of migrants, refugees, and contraband within and across Libya's largely un-policed borders. Current U.S. efforts focus on supporting the implementation of the U.N. Action Plan, preventing Libyan territory from being used to support terrorist attacks, and providing stabilization and transition assistance to local communities and national government entities. Libya's natural resources and economic potential may provide opportunities for strengthening U.S.-Libyan trade and investment ties, but circumstances have not allowed such ties to flourish.

The Trump Administration has maintained U.S. recognition of the GNA and signaled continuing interest in providing U.S. foreign aid and security assistance to support Libya's transition. Then-Ambassador to Libya Peter Bodde and AFRICOM Commander General Thomas Waldhauser visited Libya in May 2017, and GNA Prime Minister Fayez al Sarraj visited Washington, DC, in November 2017. The Trump Administration has not appointed a Special Envoy for Libya to replace Jonathan Winer, whose mandate ended with the Obama Administration. Since 2017, the Trump Administration has imposed conditional restrictions on the entry of Libyan nationals to the United States, with some exceptions.[21]

---

[19] In response to recent concerns about migrant detention and slavery, the European Union, African Union, and United Nations have established a Task Force to improve migrant protection along migration routes to, from, and in Libya. Through the Task Force, IOM has facilitated the return of more than 15,000 migrants to their home countries from Libya through a voluntary humanitarian returns program since December 2017. In parallel, the Task Force has supported UNHCR-led evacuations of more than 1,300 refugees from Libya as of March 2018.

[20] EUNAVFOR MED, "Activity updated to 19 February 2018" and, "A new Force Commander and a new flagship for SOPHIA," December 15, 2017.

[21] Libya is among the countries identified in Executive Order 13780 of March 2017, which restricts the entry of nationals of certain countries to the United States, with some exceptions. In September 2017, the Trump Administration issued further (continued...)

As noted above, the State Department suspended operations at the U.S. Embassy in Tripoli in July 2014. U.S. diplomats engage with Libyans and monitor U.S. programs in Libya via the Libya External Office (LEO) at the U.S. Embassy in Tunisia. U.S. Ambassador to Libya Peter Bodde retired in December 2017, and, as of April 16, the Trump Administration had not nominated a new Ambassador-designate. Senior Foreign Service officer Stephanie Williams leads the LEO as Chargé d'Affaires.

Diplomacy and Support for the U.N. Action Plan

U.S. officials engage in multidirectional diplomacy with parties in Libya and beyond in support of U.N.-facilitated reconciliation efforts. In a statement on December 14, 2017, the United States joined other members of the U.N. Security Council in stating that the 2015 Skhirat agreement "remains the only viable framework to end the Libyan political crisis and that its implementation remains key to holding elections and finalizing the political transition." The Council emphasized the agreement's "continuity ....throughout Libya's transitional period" and rejected "incorrect deadlines that only serve to undermine the U.N.-facilitated political process," a reference to Khalifa Haftar's statements at the time asserting the agreement's lapse. Council members further stated that "any attempt, including by Libyan parties, to undermine the Libyan-led, U.N.-facilitated political process is unacceptable."

In January 2018, U.S. Representative to the United Nations Ambassador Nikki Haley said in a Security Council meeting on Libya that:

> The United States will oppose attempts to impose a military solution to this political crisis, which would further undermine Libya's stability. Those who pursue a military solution will wind up helping terrorist groups that thrive on instability. The only legitimate path to power is through free and fair elections. ...The House of Representatives must uphold its commitment to pass laws for a constitutional referendum and for elections this year, in consultation with the High State Council. As the Libyans prepare for elections, we support United Nations efforts to promote more effective and accountable governance for this transitional period. All Libyan parties should engage constructively with the United Nations to strengthen the Libyan Political Agreement [the 2015 Skhirat agreement].

The United States and the European Union (EU) have placed financial and travel sanctions on some Libyan leaders for obstructing the implementation of the 2015 Skhirat agreement and for illicitly smuggling oil from the country.[22] In June 2017, the U.N. Security Council unanimously extended maritime arms embargo enforcement provisions for one year in Resolution 2357. The Security Council later adopted Resolution 2362—extending the mandate for maritime enforcement of oil shipment

---

(...continued)

guidance on the entry restrictions, and suspended the entry to the United States of Libyan nationals as immigrants and non-immigrants in business (B-1), tourist (B-2), and business/tourist (B-1/B-2) visa classes. The White House, Fact Sheet: Proclamation on Enhancing Vetting Capabilities and Processes for Detecting Attempted Entry into the United States by Terrorists or Other Public-Safety Threats, September 24, 2017.

[22] Executive Order 13726 (April 2016) modified U.S. sanctions enforcement measures in support of the Skhirat agreement by amending the scope of the national emergency with respect to Libya declared in Executive Order 13566 (February 2011). Under the modified measures, property under U.S. jurisdiction may be blocked and entry to the United States may be prohibited for individuals and entities found to be engaging or to have engaged in a range of actions, including threatening the peace, stability, or security of Libya and obstructing, undermining, delaying, or impeding the adoption of or transfer of power to the GNA or successor government. To date, the U.S. government has placed related sanctions on former GNC government prime minister Khalifa Ghwell and HOR leader Aqilah Issa Saleh for obstructing the implementation of the Skhirat agreement. Executive Order 13726 also provides for sanctions on individuals involved in illicit oil smuggling from Libya, and the Trump Administration used this authority in February 2018. See U.S. Department of the Treasury, "Treasury Designates Additional Libyan Political Obstructionist," May 13, 2016; and, "Treasury Sanctions International Network Smuggling Oil from Libya to Europe," February 26, 2018.

monitoring and reaffirming existing arms embargo, asset freeze, and travel ban measures.[23] U.S. naval forces interdicted an unauthorized oil shipment in 2014, and the European Union's EUNAVFOR MED mission currently monitors shipments to and from Libya. Resolution 2362 stresses "the need for the Government of National Accord to exercise sole and effective oversight over the National Oil Corporation, the Central Bank of Libya, and the Libyan Investment Authority as a matter of urgency, without prejudice to future constitutional arrangements pursuant to the Libyan Political Agreement."

Counterterrorism and Defense Policy

Transnational terrorist groups and locally organized armed extremist groups, including supporters of the Islamic State organization and Al Qaeda in the Islamic Maghreb (AQIM), remain active in Libya.[24] Some IS fighters appear to have regrouped in rural areas after fleeing Sirte in late 2016, and the group claimed a series of attacks on Libyan forces in 2017. In January 2018, a spokesperson for U.S. Africa Command (AFRICOM) projected that the Islamic State would "give priority to the restructuring of security forces and infrastructure, and to launch strikes, which may include targets in the Libyan oil crescent."[25] In March 2018 congressional testimony, AFRICOM Commander General Waldhauser described IS forces in Libya as "dispersed and disorganized and likely capable of little more than localized attacks."[26]

General Waldhauser advised Congress in March 2018 that U.S. military support for anti-IS fighters is continuing, and he emphasized the importance of political reconciliation as a prerequisite for lasting security. In this regard, AFRICOM's 2017 posture statement judged that "stability in Libya" is likely to be "a long-term proposition requiring strategic patience." The statement also advised Congress that Libya's absorption capacity for international support remains "limited," as does the ability of outsiders, including the United States, "to influence political reconciliation between competing factions." In his March 2018 testimony, General Waldhauser warned that "the risk of a full-scale civil war remains real." At present, AFRICOM describes four objectives for its approach to Libya: degrading terrorist groups; averting civil war; supporting political reconciliation with the goal of achieving a unified central government; and, helping to curb the flow of illegal migrants into Europe via Libya.

AFRICOM announced that U.S. forces conducted airstrikes against Islamic State positions south of Sirte in September and November 2017, killing IS fighters and the destroying arms and vehicles. U.S. military statements said the Islamic State used the locations targeted in September as transit hubs and operational planning centers, including for external attacks. In October 2017, U.S. forces and Libyan partner forces seized a second suspect in the 2012 Benghazi attacks in Libya, Syrian national Mustafa al Imam, near Misrata.[27] He appeared in federal court in Washington, DC, in November 2017. In March 2018, AFRICOM announced the death of AQIM senior figure Musa Abu Dawud and an associate in a U.S. airstrike near Ubari in southwest Libya.[28]

---

[23] Maritime oil shipment monitoring was first authorized in March 2014 under Security Council Resolution 2146.

[24] See CRS In Focus IF10172, *Al Qaeda in the Islamic Maghreb (AQIM) and Related Groups*, by Alexis Arieff.

[25] Robyn Mack, quoted in Al Sharq Al Awsat (London), "AFRICOM Expects ISIS Attack on Libya's Oil Crescent," January 3, 2018.

[26] U.S. AFRICOM Commander Gen. Thomas Waldhauser, Testimony before the Senate Armed Services Committee, March 13, 2018.

[27] See U.S. Department of Justice, Libyan National Charged With Federal Offenses In 2012 Attack on U.S. Special Mission and Annex in Benghazi, October 30, 2017. Mustafa al Imam pled not guilty to charges against him in November 2017. In June 2014, U.S. forces apprehended Ahmed Abu Khattala, a Libyan suspect in the attack and the reported leader of the Abu Ubaydah ibn Jarah Battalion, in a military operation in Libya and transferred him to the United States. In November 2017, he was convicted in U.S. federal court on 4 of 18 charges that had been brought against him.

[28] Abu Dawud had since 2013 been put "in charge of a mission in Tunisia tasked with recruiting and training new members from across North Africa on the use of weapons," according to a State Department release in 2016. State Department Bureau of (continued...)

President Trump's December 2017 letter to Congress consistent with the War Powers Resolution acknowledged U.S. strikes against terrorist targets in Libya. Like the Obama Administration before it, the Trump Administration has described U.S. strikes against IS and AQIM targets in Libya as authorized by the 2001 Authorization for Use of Military Force (AUMF, P.L. 107-40) and has stated that the strikes are taken "at the request and with the consent of the GNA in the context of the ongoing armed conflict against ISIL and in furtherance of U.S. national self-defense."[29]

Stabilization and Transition Support

In parallel to counterterrorism and defense policy efforts, the United States is using U.S. foreign assistance funding to support a variety of stabilization and transition assistance programs at the local and national levels in Libya. Since the 2014 withdrawal of U.S. personnel from the country, U.S. programs have been administered from outside the country. Despite related challenges, Administration officials remain committed to providing stabilization and transition support to Libyans and have notified Congress of planned aid obligations in 2017 and 2018.

Since 2016, the executive branch has notified Congress of planned programs to continue to engage with Libyan civil society organizations, support multilateral bodies engaged in Libyan stabilization efforts, and build the capacity of municipal authorities, electoral administration entities, and the emerging GNA administration. These notifications include, but are not limited to

- $64.5 million to support the continuation of USAID's Office of Transition Initiatives and other USAID good governance and electoral support programs;
- $1.9 million in Middle East Partnerships Initiative (MEPI) civil society support programming;
- $4 million for the United Nations Development Program Stabilization Facility for Libya;[30]
- $10 million for U.S. support to UNSMIL and governance programs in support of the GNA;
- $4 million for third-party monitoring of U.S. government Libya programs and for reconciliation, transitional justice, and accountability programming; and
- $10 million for training and advisory support to the GNA Ministry of Interior.

The Trump Administration has requested $34.5 million in foreign operations funding for Libya programming in FY2019 (see **Table 2** below).

Humanitarian Assistance

The United States provided more than $90 million in immediate humanitarian assistance to Libya in 2011, and U.S. assistance for humanitarian operations in Libya has ebbed and flowed in the years since in response to fluctuating needs and conditions on the ground. U.S. humanitarian funding for Libya in FY2016 and FY2017 totaled $28.325 million, more than $18 million of which was provided in FY2017.

(...continued)

Counterterrorism, "State Department Terrorist Designation of Musa Abu Dawud," May 5, 2016.

[29] Report on the Legal and Policy Frameworks Guiding the United States' Use of Military Force and Related National Security Operations, December 2016 and March 2018. See CRS Report R43983, *2001 Authorization for Use of Military Force: Issues Concerning Its Continued Application*, by Matthew C. Weed.

[30] See UNDP website: [http://www.ly.undp.org/content/libya/en/home/operations/projects/sustainable-development/stabilization-facility-for-libya.html].

This included U.S. contributions to the U.N. Office for the Coordination of Humanitarian Affairs (OCHA) Humanitarian Response Plans (HRP) for Libya and programs overseen by the State Department Bureau of Population, Refugees, and Migration (PRM) and USAID's Office of Foreign Disaster Assistance (OFDA).[31] The 2018 U.N. HRP seeks $306 million in international contributions, of which 2.1% was funded as of April 2018.[32]

Table 2. U.S. Foreign Assistance for Programs in Libya

(millions of dollars)

Account	FY2015 Actual	FY2016 Actual	FY2017 Actual	FY2018 Request	FY2019 Request
Bilateral Foreign Assistance					
Economic Support Fund (ESF/ESDF)	19.2ª	10	88	23	27
International Narcotics Control and Law Enforcement (INCLE)	1.987	2	10.2	1	1
Nonproliferation, Antiterrorism, Demining and Related Programs (NADR)	3.5	6.5	36	7	6.5
Bureau of Conflict and Stabilization Operations Funds	2.5	-	-	-	-
Peacekeeping Operations (PKO)	-	-	5	-	-
Total	**27.187**	**18.5**	**139.2**	**31**	**34.5**

Source: State Department appropriations requests and notifications FY2015-FY2018; and, Explanatory Statement for Division K of P.L. 114-113, the FY2016 Consolidated Appropriations Act.

Notes: Amounts are subject to change. Funds from centrally managed programs, including the Middle East Partnership Initiative (MEPI) and Bureau of Democracy, Human Rights and Labor (DRL) Office of Global Programming also benefit Libyans. State and USAID also use funds from the Migration and Refugee Assistance (MRA) and International Disaster Assistance (IDA) humanitarian accounts for programs in Libya.

a.   Includes ESF and ESF-OCO notified to Congress in 2016 to support Libya programs.

Congress and Libya

Congress has conditionally appropriated funding for limited U.S. transition support and security assistance programs for Libya since 2011 and is considering Trump Administration requests for additional foreign operations and defense funds to support Libya-related programs for FY2019. In recent years, Congress has enacted appropriations legislation requiring the Administration to certify Libyan cooperation with efforts to investigate the 2012 Benghazi attacks and to submit detailed spending and vetting plans to in order to obligate appropriated funds.[33] Congress also has prohibited the provision of U.S. assistance to Libya for infrastructure projects "except on a loan basis with terms favorable to the United States."

The foreign operations appropriations act for FY2018 carries forward some past terms and conditions on FY2018 U.S. assistance to Libya (Section 7041(f) of Division K of H.R. 1625/P.L.115-141), and includes a requirement for notice to Congress in cases of aid diversion or destruction. The FY2017 and FY2018

---

[31] USAID, Libya – Complex Emergency Fact Sheet #1, FY2018, December 1, 2017.

[32] U.N. Financial Tracking Service data. The 2017 appeal for $151 million was 71.3% funded by January 2018.

[33] In the FY2014, FY2015, FY2016, and FY2017 Consolidated Appropriations Acts (P.L. 113-76, Division K, Section 7041[f]; P.L. 113-235, Division J, Section 7041[f]; P.L. 114-113, Division K, Section 7041[f]; P.L. 115-31, Division J, Section 7041[g]), Congress placed conditions on the provision of funds appropriated by those acts to the central government of Libya.

acts did not require submission of a spend plan to congressional appropriators prior to obligations. Division B of the December 2016 continuing resolution (P.L. 114-254) provided additional overseas contingency operations assistance and operations funding to the State Department and USAID, some of which is supporting post-IS stabilization efforts in Libya and may facilitate the eventual return of U.S. government personnel to the country.

Outlook

At present, U.S. officials remain engaged with Libyan counterparts in efforts to move forward with the U.N.-backed Action Plan. Next steps may include a constitutional referendum and national elections some time in 2018 or later, but the timing, legal framework, and sequencing of these proposed steps has not yet been determined. The potential success of U.N.-backed reconciliation could provide a new foundation for improving stability in Libya, and could create new opportunities for security and economic partnership between Libya and the United States. The potential failure of U.N.-promoted reconciliation efforts among Libyans may present U.S. decisionmakers with hard choices about how best to mitigate threats emanating from the country in the continuing absence of a viable, legitimate national government. Possible questions before the United States may include

- whether and when to return U.S. personnel to Libya on a permanent basis;
- what types and extent of assistance, if any, to provide for stabilization and transition support purposes;
- how to ensure that U.S. aid recipients and security partners have not been and are not now involved in gross violations of human rights;
- whether or how to use existing sanctions provisions or other coercive measures against parties seen as obstructing progress under the U.N.-sponsored Action Plan;
- whether or how to continue to intervene militarily against terrorist groups;
- whether or how to respond to the actions of other third parties, including Russia;
- whether or how to leverage or amend U.N. arms embargo provisions to allow for security assistance to parties in Libya;
- what degree of support, if any, to provide to emergent national security forces (particularly in the absence of an agreed political framework); and
- whether or how to respond in the event of any military clashes between rival Libyan factions that involve groups that have received U.S. assistance.

Legislative debates over future appropriations and defense authorization measures provide potential means for Members to influence U.S. policy and engagement with Libyan actors. Congressional oversight prerogatives also provide opportunities to engage Administration officials

- to refine the scope and content of U.S. programs proposed to support the Government of National Accord and other Libyans;
- regarding U.S. contingency planning for the possibility that other third parties may intervene more forcefully in Libya;
- regarding plans for potentially expanding U.S. partnership with Libyans if U.N.-backed reconciliation measures succeed; and
- regarding the possibility that negotiations among Libyans and planned elections may not bring instability in Libya to a prompt close.

This concludes my statement; thank you for the opportunity to testify, and I look forward to your questions.

Ms. ROS-LEHTINEN. Thank you very much.
Dr. Wehrey?

STATEMENT OF FREDERIC WEHREY, PH.D., SENIOR FELLOW, MIDDLE EAST PROGRAM, CARNEGIE ENDOWMENT FOR INTERNATIONAL PEACE

Mr. WEHREY. Thank you. Chairman Ros-Lehtinen, Ranking Member Deutch, members of the subcommittee, it is a privilege to speak with you here today about Libya's ongoing struggle for stability, peace, and unity.

I join you, having visited western Libya in December of last year, where I glimpsed firsthand the severity of the challenges, the growing power of its predatory armed groups and the criminal networks, the plunder of its economy, the potential re-emergence of radicalism, to name but a few. Underpinning all of these inflictions is the weakness of governing institutions and national political fissures.

I will start with my visit to the central coastal city of Sirte, the object of intense American focus in 2016 during the war against the Islamic State. While the Islamic State was ousted from its stronghold there at the cost of over 700 Libyan lives, Sirte faces daunting challenges of reconstruction and recovery. Bridging the social damage wrought by the Islamic State's divisive rule is especially crucial, as is restoring law and order.

Though the Islamic State has dispersed to the desert southwest of the city, it is still potent. It could easily exploit Libya's political divisions and the unwillingness of armed groups to confront it. We have seen this before where Libya's opposing factions where so focused on battling each other that they ignored the growing radical presence in their midst. That is why national-level reconciliation is so important, along with unifying and reforming the security sector.

Another important component of reform lies in the judicial and penal sector. Arbitrary detentions, torture, and killings in militia-run prisons is a potential time bomb for radicalism. In one such prison that I visited, suspected Islamic State fighters are detained in the same facility as petty criminals and drug addicts, along with the political rivals of the militias.

And, of course, the militia-run detention centers for migrants are a wholly different moral tragedy. Thousands of migrants are kept in these horrific conditions, which I saw firsthand, and many of these detention centers, of course, are run by militias affiliated with the Government of National Accord. All this must change.

Though security conditions in the absence of a diplomatic presence have constrained our ability to engage, there are still plentiful opportunities, especially at the level of municipal governance. Elected city councils in Libya are one of the country's bright spots. In many cases, they enjoy strong legitimacy and they have been engines for reconciliation in a way that national actors have not. American aid and assistance to municipalities is, therefore, a worthy investment.

But municipal governance is hampered by corruption in national economic institutions. Libya is afflicted by a culture of entitlement by its armed groups, many of whom, as I have mentioned, are affiliated with the government. The plunder of Libya's Central Bank adds to the income that these groups already get from illicit activities like smuggling, fuel smuggling and human trafficking. A lasting fix to this problem requires sustained American diplomatic engagement with officials from the Central Bank and other economic institutions.

Now all of these challenges I have outlined hinge upon progress on the political front, on national reconciliation. The U.S. and its partners must continue to play a strong convening and persuading role, especially among its regional Arab allies and, also, the Europeans to support the U.N.-led roadmap. The U.N.-led roadmap is currently headed toward convening national Presidential and parliamentary elections. This shows that Libyans have not given up on a democracy, despite the turmoil of the past year. However, a word of caution is in order. Elections by themselves, if they are held hastily without a constitutional framework, risk a return to strife. We have seen this before in the past in 2012 and in 2014.

Thank you for the opportunity to speak with you here today.

[The prepared statement of Mr. Wehrey follows:]

CARNEGIE
ENDOWMENT FOR
INTERNATIONAL PEACE

Congressional Testimony

Libya Fractured: The Struggle for Unity

Frederic Wehrey
Senior Fellow,
Middle East Program
Carnegie Endowment for International Peace

Testimony before U.S. House of Representatives
Subcommittee on the Middle East and North
Africa (Committee on Foreign Affairs)

April 18, 2018

Chairman Ros-Lehtinen, Ranking Member Deutch, members of the subcommittee, it is a privilege to speak with you here today about Libya's ongoing struggle for stability, peace, and unity. I join you having visited western Libya in December of last year where I glimpsed firsthand the severity of the challenges the country faces: the growing power of its predatory armed groups and criminal networks, the plunder of its economy, and the potential for a re-emergence of radical militancy, to name but a few. Underpinning all of these afflictions is the weakness of governing institutions and a deterioration of basic services, which creates an incentive and justification for unscrupulous local actors like militia bosses to fill the void. Added to this is a yawning, national-level political divide, and continued meddling by outside states, to include the entry of fighters and weapons in contravention of the UN arms embargo.

Let me elaborate on some of the gravest hurdles Libya faces and ways that the United States can assist.

I'll start with my visit to a place that was the object of intense American focus last year in the campaign against the Islamic State, the central coastal city of Sirte. While the Islamic State was ousted from its stronghold there in December 2016, at the cost of over 700 Libyan lives, Sirte faces the daunting task of reconstruction and recovery. More than a year after its liberation, vast swathes of its downtown lie in rubble and displaced residents are furious at the Tripoli government's glacial response. While the United Nations Development Program has appropriately identified Sirte as the beneficiary of a sweeping aid effort, more remains to be done. Bridging the social fissures wrought by the Islamic State's divisive rule is especially crucial, as is restoring law and order.

The aftermath of Sirte also raises the question of the Islamic State's potential reemergence. Based on my discussions with Libyan officials, the Islamic State has fled to the desert southwest of the city where it remains dispersed, but still potent. It could easily exploit Libya's political divisions and the inability or unwillingness of Libya's armed groups to confront it. We have seen this before, when Libya's opposing factions were so focused on battling one another that they ignored the growing radical presence in their midst. This is why national level political reconciliation is so important, along with unifying and reforming the security sector.

Even further south, in the southwest corner of Libya near the Algerian border, extremists have a presence around the town of Ubari, where the United States conducted an airstrike last month against al-Qaeda. Transnational jihadists have exploited weak administration, porous border control, and economic despair to use the area as a logistic hub. But people in Ubari told me during a visit that the penetration of radicalism into their community is shallow and that any support for the jihadists is often highly transactional and opportunistic. So, here again, a lasting solution for the challenge of militancy lies in better governance and economic opportunities, which also holds true across southern Libya. The United States can play a role by redoubling its development assistance and supporting UN-led efforts, but also exercising greater leverage on the governments of Libya's Sahelian neighbors, who need to do more to stop the flow of fighters and illicit goods across their borders.

Another important component to denying the extremists space to remerge lies in the judicial and penal sector. As a recent United Nations report made shockingly clear, the widespread practice of arbitrary detentions, torture, and killings in militia-run prisons is a potential space for breeding radicalism. The fact that some of these prisons are nominally "official" or quasi-official does nothing to lessen the gravity of the abuses. There is often minimal or non-existent due process in these cases: the prisoners are released at the whim of the militia wardens, if they are ever released at all. This must change.

While combatting extremism in Libya is important, this should not be the sole lens through which America views the country. Libyans I met in the city of Benghazi and across the country still recall with fondness the well-meaning efforts of American diplomats, especially the late Ambassador Chris Stevens, to engage with civil society groups and support Libyans in areas like education, citizenship, and media. While security conditions and the absence of an American diplomatic presence have constrained our ability to do this, there are still plentiful opportunities, especially at the level of municipalities.

City- and town-level governance in many areas is one of Libya's rare bright spots: Libyans like to say that since national institutions are moribund and frozen in political conflict, it is up to elected town councils and mayors to manage on their own. And in many cases they enjoy strong legitimacy and have proven to be engines for reconciliation in a way that national actors are not, holding meetings with other towns to coordinate on shared economic and political interests. American support to municipalities is therefore a worthy investment in Libya's future. Yet development at the town level is hampered by Libya's endemic budgetary problems, which in turn are tied to corruption in national economic institutions.

Libya's oil revenues are high, but the resulting revenue is not reaching the average Libyan in terms of better services. Libya's financial institutions remain divided and beset by administrative shortfalls, namely the absence of a budget. But most important, Libya is afflicted by a culture of entitlement and predation by Libya's armed groups, many of whom claim affiliation with the internationally recognized Government of National Accord. Acting as quasi-police, the funds diverted to these armed groups go well beyond salaries to members, including letters of credit from the Central Bank. The plunder of the Central Bank adds to the income these groups already derive from illicit activities like fuel smuggling and human trafficking. A lasting fix to this phenomenon requires sustained American diplomatic engagement with officials at the Central Bank and other institutions.

Sustained engagement ultimately means an American diplomatic return to the capital and the appointment of an Ambassador. In an encouraging sign, the United Nations has returned, and a number of other countries have either a permanent or rotating diplomatic presence. Yet as I saw last winter, security in Tripoli remains tenuous: the weak uniformed police conduct checkpoints and patrols but lack vital equipment like body armor, patrol cars, and a forensics capability. But more importantly, they are at the mercy of better-armed militias who control specific neighborhoods. These militias, of course, sometimes have their own agendas that diverge sharply from the enforcement of codified law, and their spontaneous clashes over power, money, and turf mean that Tripoli's outward appearance of peace is often illusory.

Libyan officials rely upon armed groups for security and international actors rely upon them for tasks ranging from counter-terrorism to countering migrant trafficking. Such reliance, however, is a Faustian bargain: cooperation with militias on these immediate international concerns inflates their authority, which in turn undermines the Libyan government and perpetuates a cycle of instability.

International engagement on countering migrant smuggling is a particular concern: militias have often competed for access to state funds, and some former smugglers, when persuaded to abandon human trafficking, have simply switched to other illicit activity. Similarly, the enmeshment of militias in government police forces presents dilemmas for outside countries wishing to assist Libya's policing sector. The United Nations has instituted a policing assistance program that deserves American support, as does the European Union and a number of countries. But diligence is important, especially in vetting and proper training on rule of law and due process.

Beyond the police, Libya needs a uniformed national army. This has been an elusive goal ever since the revolution, when Libyans and their Western supporters were struggling with the legacy of Qadhafi's policy of neglecting the army, which left it a hollow and decrepit institution with a top-heavy rank structure. Adding to this challenge was the mushrooming of better-armed militias with access to state funds who opposed the creation of an army. Virtually every international effort to train and equip the Libyan army or reform its bureaucratic capability has foundered, principally because Libyans remain divided about the organization of the army and, crucially, the inclusion of armed groups. Limited and well-meaning training programs resulted in Libyan soldiers returning to Libya to find no defined army structure to join and often melting back to their town or militia. America and its NATO partners—Italy, Britain and Turkey—learned this painful lesson with the aborted General Purpose Force (GPF) program that began in 2013. To avoid a repeat of this episode, the U.S. should desist from any further training or assistance to the Libyan army until Libyans reach a political consensus among the various armed groups and develop an agreed-upon roadmap for disarming and demobilizing the militias.

All of these challenges I've outlined above hinge upon progress on the political front and on national reconciliation. Here, the U.S. must play a strong diplomatic role, particularly in persuading regional states to support the United Nations-led roadmap, which is crucial to prevent spoilers from disrupting the process. The United Nations has made amendments to the Libyan Political Agreement its priority and is also moving toward a national dialogue conference. It is also ready to support Libya's establishment of a strong legal framework through a constitution, which is vital to ending Libya's transition period. Finally, it is assisting in the convening of national presidential and parliamentary elections—an event that underscores Libyans' continued support for participatory politics, despite the turmoil of the past years.

Here, however, a word of caution is in order. If held hastily or without the presence of a constitutional framework, adequate security, and voting laws, elections risk a return to strife, either through the actions of spoilers or by producing yet another governing body that does not enjoy buy-in and is seen as transitional. We have seen Libyans' hopes for elections dashed in the past—in 2012 after the General National Congress elections and again in 2014 after voting for the House or Representatives, which both produced factional conflict in their aftermath. It is crucial to remember, therefore, that elections by themselves are not a panacea or a default fallback when other mechanisms are stuck.

Let me close with a few thoughts on Benghazi, a name that looms large in the American mind because of the tragedy of September 11th and 12th, 2012, which took the lives of four brave Americans. The Libyans I've met, especially in Benghazi, remember that night with sadness and regret, yet they are eager for America to move beyond the shadow of the attack. Benghazi, they would like to remind us, is also Libya's second largest city, home to a rich culture and distinguished history that includes the Libyan drive for independence and, crucially, the Libyan struggle against Qadhafi. After that struggle, however, the city fell into neglect and violence, which the period after the 2012 attack and the departure of the international community only worsened. The city then saw three plus years of non-stop warfare, which displaced thousands and ruptured its social fabric.

Libyans in the city are therefore relishing a return to normalcy and are eager for the return of internationals and an American presence. America's interactions in the east, however, must be predicated on inclusive and democratic governance and not on one person or faction. The hospitalization of a central figure in Benghazi's recent history, General Khalifa Hiftar, who led a military campaign in the city against Islamists and other militias and then jockeyed for national political power, underscores the fallibility of placing too much stock in one personality. Hiftar's military coalition was always more divided than was commonly assumed, with tribes, militias, and religious actors attaching themselves to his operation for their own localized and self-interested goals. A diminishing of his influence or his disappearance from the scene could thrust eastern Libya into a new phase of uncertainty but also presents opportunities for renewed American diplomacy.

It is true that Libya is often overshadowed by a host of other crises and challenges that demand America's attention. But the country remains a place of great potential and resilience and it affects our interests and those of our European partners, beyond the threat of terrorism. I urge the subcommittee to support a durable strategy to helping this country realize the promise of its revolution.

Thank you for the opportunity to speak with you here today.

———————

Ms. Ros-Lehtinen. Thank you so much, Doctor.

Ms. Friend?

STATEMENT OF MS. ALICE HUNT FRIEND, SENIOR FELLOW, INTERNATIONAL SECURITY PROGRAM, CENTER FOR STRATEGIC AND INTERNATIONAL STUDIES

Ms. Friend. Chairman Ros-Lehtinen, Ranking Member Deutch, members of the committee, distinguished colleagues, it is my pleasure to be here today to discuss the current situation in Libya.

The complexity of the civil war in Libya is rivaled only by the complexity of the related crisis it breeds. The diversity and ferocity of the country's domestic politics create obstacles for terrorists attempting to establish havens, but also make the role of Islam in governance a central and contentious object of Libyan politics, amplifying Libya's salience to global Islamic terrorism. Libya's oil resources, proximity to Europe, and cultural connections to the Middle East make it a strategic prize for multiple powerful outside actors, and its competing governments and myriad militias fuel an international race for Libyan proxies. In the midst of it all, an historic volume of migrants is coming through Libya, fleeing into the Mediterranean, overwhelming European and broader international resources.

Ending major violence and stabilizing Libyan politics to the point where powerful actors accept a single government will be the most durable way to address terrorism and humanitarian needs. Yet, the path to political equilibrium will likely be a long one. The international community, including the United States, should have a patient and realistic approach to Libyan politics that also accounts for Libyan internal security concerns.

The current challenge for the U.S. is knowing whom and how to engage among the constantly shifting array of power brokers and would-be national leaders to encourage political accommodations and meaningfully address the humanitarian crisis. The reported incapacitation of the Libyan National Army command and the east-dominant center of power, Khalifa Haftar, is likely to generate some political and security realignments if Haftar is unable to return to the country.

Although group alignments with the U.N.-backed Government of National Accord should open the door to outsider engagement in principle, the persistent dynamism of Libyan politics recommends a cautious approach to security assistance. Even if the policy remains largely focused on countering ISIS and al-Qaeda, the U.S. will need to determine ways to sustain pressure on terrorist groups without undermining the prospects for Libya's stability.

With regard to ongoing U.S. efforts to disrupt and dismantle ISIS's operations in Libya, I believe the current offshore pressure campaign and counterterrorism capacity-building efforts among Libya's neighbors strikes the right balance between U.S. national security and the prospects for Libyan stability.

Given the range of crises consuming American policymakers' time, it seems likely that U.S. efforts in Libya overall will remain relatively modest, but continued negotiations and implementation of the Libyan Political Agreement are best accomplished with the support of the U.S., not only in a diplomatic sense and by eventually assisting the development of national security forces, but also in a role supporting U.N. Security Council prohibitions on disrupting constructive intra-Libyan balances of power. This latter effort requires deft diplomacy, especially with Gulf partners and Russia, given the issue linkages elsewhere, but it would be the kind of international leadership only the U.S. can provide.

Thank you again for calling us together today, and I look forward to your questions.

[The prepared statement of Ms. Friend follows:]

CSIS | CENTER FOR STRATEGIC &
INTERNATIONAL STUDIES

Statement Before the

House Committee on Foreign Affairs

Subcommittee on the Middle East and North Africa

"Libya Fractured: The Struggle for Unity"

A Testimony by:

Alice Hunt Friend

Senior Fellow

Center for Strategic and International Studies

April 18, 2018

2172 Rayburn House Office Building

WWW.CSIS.ORG   1616 RHODE ISLAND AVENUE NW | TEL. (202) 887.0200
WASHINGTON, DC 20036 | FAX (202) 775.3199

Introduction

The complexity of the civil war in Libya is rivaled only by the complexity of the related crises it breeds. The diversity and ferocity of the country's domestic politics create obstacles for terrorists attempting to establish havens, but also make the role of Islam in governance a central and contentious object of Libyan politics, amplifying Libya's salience to global Islamist terrorism. Libya's oil resources, proximity to Europe, and cultural connections to the Middle East make it a strategic prize for multiple powerful outside actors, and its three competing governments and myriad militias fuel an international race for Libyan proxies that includes Russia, Turkey, Egypt, the Gulf States, and others. In the midst of it all, an historic volume of migrants is coming both from and through Libya, fleeing into the Mediterranean and overwhelming European and broader international resources.

Ending major violence and stabilizing Libyan politics to the point where powerful actors accept a single government will be the most durable way to address terrorism and humanitarian needs. Yet the path to political equilibrium will likely be longer than one U.S. presidential term. The international community, including the United States, will have to adopt a patient and realistic approach to Libyan politics that also accounts for Libyan internal security concerns. The current challenge for the U.S. is knowing whom and how to engage among the constantly-shifting array of power brokers and would-be national leaders to encourage political accommodations and meaningfully address the humanitarian crisis. Even if the policy remains narrowly focused on countering terrorism and, within that category, ISIS and al Qaeda in particular, the U.S. will need to determine ways to sustain pressure on terrorist groups without undermining the prospects for Libya's stability.

The Dynamics of Libya's Civil War: Critical Events and Key Players

It has been said that a state is defined by its ability to monopolize the legitimate control of violence within its own territory.[1] Typically, this occurs by marrying rule of law to a national armed force subordinate to state control and able to operate throughout the country. Contemporary Libya, however, is an amalgam of dozens of political groups and hundreds of militias engaged in civil war characterized by competition for urban centers and provincial territorial blocs.

The international community has attempted to forge unity among Libya's various competing groups.[2] But it is useful to keep in mind that unity across the three main regions of Libya would be an historical anomaly, something imposed only fleetingly by external actors and artificially by the country's late dictator, Muamar Qaddafi. Moreover, in states with a population that is heterogeneous along multiple axes, regardless of domestic unrest, the notion of unity is not

---

[1] Max Weber. 1946. "Politics as a Vocation." In *Essays in Sociology*, ed. H.H. Garth and C.W. Mills. New York: Macmillian.

[2] The European Council on Foreign Relations' Mattia Toaldo put together a helpful compendium in his "A Quick Guide to Libya's Main Players" accessible at: http://www.ecfr.eu/mena/mapping_libya_conflict. For an excellent summary of Islamist groups, see Cameron Glenn. "Libya's Islamists: Who They Are – And What They Want." Woodrow Wilson Center. August 8, 2017. https://www.wilsoncenter.org/article/libyas-islamists-who-they-are-and-what-they-want

as useful as the concept of coalition.[3] A coalition links together a variety of actors with similar, but not necessarily identically overlapping, goals. The mechanism that creates a coalition combines power and opportunity: Where actors and groups see benefits to their own power in given circumstances, they will ally with others. And in civil war, until one coalition manages to accumulate the preponderance of power—or power distributes equally among a small number of groups to the point of stalemate—the fighting will endure, and coalitions will continue to splinter and realign.

Recent History

Beginning soon after the rebel victory in the uprisings of 2011, clashes among and between regionally based militias that never disarmed after Qaddafi's ouster marked struggles for political autonomy within the nascent national framework. Throughout 2012 and 2013, networks of militias centered around the eastern city of Benghazi and the western city of Zintan built power and influence among emerging political parties, effectively preventing nationwide security institutions from developing.

In 2014, the mandate for the Tripoli-based General National Congress (GNC) expired with no clear successor organization. A vacuum of national legitimacy gave way to increased struggles for power in the Tripolitania and Cyrenaica regions, and disputed elections over the summer did nothing to resolve tensions. The government split in two, with the Islamist-dominated GNC in Tripoli and an internationally-recognized House of Representatives (HoR) in the far eastern city of Tobruk. That same year, a former Libyan army general named Khalifa Haftar organized the Libyan National Army (LNA) in opposition to the Islamist militias running Benghazi. Eventually given formal command of the armed forces by the HoR, Haftar became a major military and political power center in his own right, with rumored designs on control of national governance. By the end of 2015, the UN had brokered a new Government of National Accord (GNA), headed by a Presidential Council initially based in Tunisia but eventually moving to Tripoli. However, large elements of both the GNC and the HoR refused to recognize this third government, and the process for the integration of the three governments has stalled.

Meanwhile, the Islamic State saw an opening. Beginning in the port of Derna and expanding into Sirte, the group proceeded with its infamously brutal tactics, including releasing a video of group members beheading 21 Coptic Christians. From the end of 2014 to mid-2017, Egypt, Misratan militias, Haftar's LNA, and the United States all mounted campaigns against ISIS' Libyan affiliate, eventually driving organized elements from Sirte, Derna, and Benghazi and into the southwestern Fezzan province.[4]

Thus, in the post-2011 confusion around national governance, still-armed militias gathered power and territory, and coalesced around particular actors and regions. After 2014, one

---

[3] My views are greatly shaped by the work of Fontini Christia's excellent 2012 book, Alliance Formation in Civil Wars. New York: Cambridge University Press.

[4] For more on the dynamics in Fezzan, see International Crisis Group's report, "How Libya's Fezzan Became Europe's New Border." Middle East and North Africa Report No. 179, July 31, 2017. https://www.crisisgroup.org/middle-east-north-africa/north-africa/libya/179-how-libyas-fezzan-became-europes-new-border

government became three, with varying attachments to Islam, secularism, and militia loyalists but none with a national military or the ability to impose legal authority over the entirety of Libya. Nor has any one figure or organization been able to amass enough power to either attract or compel de-facto national-level loyalty. This has meant not only ongoing and violent struggles for federal power, but also frequent re-alignments among power blocs in attempts to generate such authority and control. It has also meant that ISIS and al Qaeda are just two fish in a sea of violent groups, and that the fight against them has tended to involve a mix of militia campaigns, Haftar's LNA, and unilateral outsider action rather than pressure directed from any of the governing centers of the country.

Dynamics Today

Today, a coalition of politicians in the Presidential Council of the GNA bring together Misratan, Zintani, Petroleum Facilities Guard, and other armed groups and political parties (including the Muslim Brotherhood). Recognized by the international community, the GNA is an alignment of actors who might compete more openly with each other absent greater threats outside the architecture of the GNA. For example, Haftar and the GNA's Minister of Defense, Mahdi al-Barghathi, are political rivals.

At the same time, the protracted and fractured nature of the conflict has generated both demand for outside assistance and opportunities for strategic advantage among international actors. Libya's proximity to Europe and Mediterranean ports, its borders with Egypt and sub-Saharan African countries, its energy resources and its Muslim population all attract a variety of outsiders. Of chief concern to the U.S. is ISIS' enduring toehold in Libya, the spillover of the Gulf crisis into Libyan proxy competition, and Russia's overtures to Libyan power brokers.

First, North African states have long-term connections to global Islamism and to the Arab world, both of which made Libya a natural outlet for ISIS militants. It also has historic connections with civilizations south of the Sahara and links al Qaeda's Sahelian affiliates with access to illicit economic opportunities and strategic depth away from both the Algerian government and Western counterterrorism forces. Although a combination of Misratan militia attacks and U.S. airstrikes drove ISIS from its coastal enclave in Sirte in 2016 while Haftar's LNA conducted an unrelated offensive against ISIS and other groups in Benghazi, the Islamic State is still a scattered presence in the East and South, and the commander of Africa Command testified that the U.S. conducted eight strikes against ISIS targets in late 2017 and early 2018.[5]

Regional rivalries also have an outlet in Libya. Egypt plays two sides of the war, formally recognizing and rhetorically supporting the UN's efforts via the GNA but materially supporting the Tobruk government and Haftar. It appears that Egypt's endgame is to generate enough independence in the anti-Islamist government in the east to stave off Muslim Brotherhood encroachments near Egyptian territory, but also to allow stability in the west and avoid international diplomatic difficulties. The United Arab Emirates have also been known to provide

---

[5] General Thomas Waldhauser, House Armed Services Committee Hearing, "National Security Challenges and U.S. Military Activities in Africa," March 6, 2018. https://armedservices.house.gov/legislation/hearings/national-security-challenges-and-us-military-activities-africa

weapons to both GNA-affiliated militias and Haftar. The GNA enjoys unmitigated support from Qatar, and a limited relationship exists between the GNC and Turkey, which also supports the GNA.

Finally, Russia has long made efforts to influence both the outcome of the domestic struggle for power and the ultimate holder of that power. Although there are allegations of various Russian efforts to arm militias in exchange for oil and other favors, Russia (or Russian actors)[6] seem to have put many of their chips on Haftar—a move now complicated by Haftar's ambiguous but apparently serious health condition taking him out of Libya entirely for the time being.[7] Like the Egyptians, Russia has also made overtures to the leader of the GNA's Presidential Council, Fayez al-Serraj. It seems clear that access is Russia's highest priority in Libya, with little principle attached to the ultimate outcome of the civil war.

The United States, for its part, has generally tried to support whichever government has the backing of the UN. As the security situation in Libya deteriorated throughout 2013 and 2014, and the American Embassy finally withdrew along with many other international missions in Tripoli, Washington's practical ability to implement assistance programs was also reduced, although it continues to conduct its diplomatic and assistance efforts from neighboring Tunisia. U.S. Africa Command made various attempts over the course of the Obama administration to bolster the security capacity of forces allied with the internationally recognized government.[8] AFRICOM has stated that efforts to help build the GNA's security capacity have continued into the Trump administration, although recent press reporting suggests there has been a temporary halt to all "military" assistance.[9]

The challenge for outside sponsors, especially those trying to enable security forces through equipping, is that both success and failure risk undermining durable political equilibria. Externally sponsored military success can mean domestic groups outpace the growth of their political legitimacy, empowering a leader or group whose goals and relationships might not otherwise allow them to achieve broad-based influence. In such a case, groups are not positioned to command national authority credibly. On the other hand, failure can simply spin wheels or freeze a conflict in place.

Humanitarian Consequences

The political ambiguity and violent undercurrents in Libya have taken a toll on its citizenry. Human Rights Watch has reported that ongoing struggles between militia blocs have led to an

---

[6] Jo Becker and Eric Schmitt. "As Trump Wavers on Libya, an ISIS Haven, Russia Presses On. The New York Times, February 7. 2018. https://www.nytimes.com/2018/02/07/world/africa/trump-libya-policy-russia.html

[7] As of this writing, Haftar's condition is still unclear, although sporadic reports of his death in a Paris hospital over the weekend of April 14th and 15th appear to be have been incorrect.

[8] Defense Security Cooperation Agency New Release. "Libya – General Purpose Force Training." January 22, 2014. http://www.dsca.mil/sites/default/files/mas/libya_13-74.pdf and Missy Ryan. "U.S. Establishes Libyan Outposts with Eye Toward Offensive Against Islamic State." *Washington Post*, May 12, 2016.

[9] Jack Detsch. "U.S. Freezes Military Aid to Chaotic Libya." *Al-Monitor*, April 10. 2018. https://www.al-monitor.com/pulse/originals/2018/04/us-freeze-military-aid-chaotic-libya.html

environment of impunity for violence, degrading major social and legal services across the country, and displacing more than 200,000 Libyans.[10]

More visible to Western audiences has been the trans-Mediterranean migration crisis. Libya has long been a transit country for migrants originating south of the Sahara Desert. Using many of the same ancient caravan routes across present-day Mali, Algeria, Niger, and Chad as those smuggling weapons, drugs, fuel, cigarettes, and other black-market goods, migratory populations aimed for Libyan ports as their penultimate destination prior to crossing into Europe.[11] Domestic resentment in Libya pushed Qaddafi's government toward draconian suppression measures and set a precedent for discounting migrants' human rights.

Since 2011, law enforcement is less of an impediment to crossing through Libya but migrants face greater danger. They are at the mercy of their traffickers, and are often abused, with little access to food or water. Most repugnant, CNN and other news organizations revealed last fall that many have become prey to a slavery economy.[12] European policy for many years has focused on maritime operations with the goals of saving those attempting transit in non-seaworthy craft and repatriating those ineligible for asylum back to North Africa. With the EU brokering a more pointed agreement with the GNA in 2017 to build Libyan capacity to keep migrants from escaping Libyan shores, the number of people successfully completing the crossing has dropped considerably,[13] meaning that a growing population of displaced Africans challenges the legal authority and humanitarian interests of the array of Libyan governing factions.[14]

Possible Resolutions

Given their contentious history, the major players in Libya do not trust each other enough to allow the vulnerability that cooperation and eventual disarmament—or at least, centralization of arms into national institutions—requires. Yet absent compromise and nationwide coalition-building, the only solution to the problem of violent competition is stalemate at best and more violence at worst. If a compromise has a chance of lasting, it must address mutual security vulnerabilities and generate a legitimate architecture for national security services.

There is no immediate reason this cannot be achieved under the framework of the 2015 Libyan Political Agreement, which established the GNA and calls for a variety of desirable security arrangements, to be implemented by the temporary security committee. What is less clear is how Libya will make the leap from fractured, militia-based security to the national army and

---

[10] Human Rights Watch World Report 2018. "Libya" https://www.hrw.org/world-report/2018/country-chapters/libya
[11] Hein de Haas. "Trans-Saharan Migration to North Africa and the EU: Historical Roots and Current Trends." https://www.migrationpolicy.org/article/trans-saharan-migration-north-africa-and-eu-historical-roots-and-current-trends
[12] Nima Elbagir, et al. "People for Sale" CNN Video: https://www.cnn.com/2017/11/14/africa/libya-migrant-auctions/index.html and David D. Kirkpatrick. "Europe Wanted Migrants Stopped. Now Some are Being Sold as Slaves." *The New York Times*, November 30, 2017.
[13] Claudia Gazzini. "Quick Fixes Won't Block Libya's People Smugglers for Long." International Crisis Group Commentary, September 14, 2017. https://www.crisisgroup.org/middle-east-north-africa/north-africa/libya/quick-fixes-wont-block-libyas-people-smugglers-long
[14] Elizabeth Collett. "New EU Partnerships in North Africa: Potential to Backfire?" Migration Policy Institute Commentary, February 2017. https://www.migrationpolicy.org/news/new-eu-partnerships-north-africa-potential-backfire

police forces laid out in the agreement. Myriad arrangements and assurances must be made to incentivize armed groups to reorganize under new institutions and leadership. Given that Haftar himself recently declared the LPA null and void, such incentives are clearly not uniformly in place.

Still, such a transition is a possible dream. Militias are already inclined to align with powerful politicians and cooperate with each other when beneficial. UN-led talks on the security sector are further proof that coalition-building is possible. The question is whether the GNA can manage a true integration of the myriad militias. Given developments over the past 18 months or so, continued coalition building among armed groups and political parties may need to continue within regions before a cooperative trans-regional architecture is possible. Much depends on what happens in the east without Haftar. Regardless, any transition from militias to an army and police force should be slow and proceed in phases, taking care to sequence the major urban areas and their affiliated militia groups on their own timelines.

Available Options for U.S. Policy

Continued negotiations and implementation of the LPA is best accomplished with the support of the U.S., not only as a direct enabler of a national army and police force through its assistance, but also in a role supporting UN Security Council resolutions prohibiting outside actors from disrupting constructive intra-Libyan balances of power. This latter effort would require deft diplomacy, especially with Gulf partners and Russia given the issue linkages elsewhere. But it would be the kind of international leadership only the U.S. can provide.

If the administration chooses to maintain its narrow policy focus on disrupting and dismantling ISIS' operations in Libya, then there is little else it can do beyond the current offshore pressure campaign and its counterterrorism capacity-building efforts among Libya's neighbors. Given the wide range of actors and their constantly shifting political fortunes, DoD is limited in the possible depths and breadth of its Libyan relationships at present. Military officials must take special care about empowering local groups at the wrong moment for national coalition-building purposes. Given the LPA's strong orientation against terrorism, the U.S. has an enduring interest in doing what it can to help the resulting government succeed—even if only by doing it no harm.

Ms. ROS-LEHTINEN. Well, thank you very much. Excellent testimony. We are very grateful for it.

I wanted to follow up on something that I had said in my opening statement about Haftar and his health. We have discussed the power struggles between the west and the east, the GNA and the LNA, and how external actors back different factions. With the uncertainty around Haftar, this raises serious questions about the direction in which Libya may go if he is incapacitated. And we may have already seen the first bit of fallout this very afternoon, as news reports indicate that the general's chief of staff survived a car bomb today in Benghazi.

So, if you could tell us what the implications could be for the political process and for Libya's security if the general is out of the picture—and, of course, we don't know that—or perceived to be weakened? Of course, Haftar's health scare, and the uncertainty that brings, also calls into question the U.N. Envoy in Libya's efforts and assertion just last month that he believes Libya is still on track to have elections before the year is out. I think that was more aspirational than realistic, but it does raise questions about the U.N. support mission in Libya and the Special Representative's role in all of this, and it also underscores the lack of a role the United States has thus far played in Libya. Can the U.N. effort be successful without the United States leadership in Libya? And how could the U.S. use our leverage to bring the external actors together to support the U.N. effort to seek political reconciliation?

And as you know, last month the Foreign Affairs Committee passed House Resolution 644 strongly condemning the slave auctions that Mr. Deutch talked about of migrants and refugees in Libya. This is, obviously, a major concern and a reprehensible human rights issue. But I was hoping we could get a better understanding of the trafficking picture and the actors involved. Who is responsible for detaining migrants and refugees in Libya? Are there outside actors involved? How do they come in? How do they operate? What role do the Libyan factions play in all of this, and how can Congress and the U.S. do more to help this awful situation?

You can tackle one or all of them, as you see fit, whichever one is your favorite. Mr. Blanchard?

Mr. BLANCHARD. That is a rich agenda. I will try to proceed through those quickly.

I think the danger in the East is a vacuum, both political and military, as we have seen or are observing, and you are hearing more about what is behind Haftar, right? The LNA is a coalition. And so, from a security standpoint, that is quite true. The different forces would need to select new leadership and that could get messy.

With regard to politics, Haftar's personal ambitions, although not directly and often clearly stated, are a sticking point in the negotiations. His desire, at a minimum, to lead the security forces, if not play a political role in the future, has been a sticking point. And so, his removal could, arguably, create an opportunity in that regard.

In terms of the role of the U.N. mission and the United States, I think it is helpful to think about the role that the U.S. plays with the U.N. as setting a floor. Our role in the Security Council, our vote and diplomacy there with regard to things like the arms embargo and things like assets is the quiet backstop to what the U.N. mission is trying to do.

In addition, our diplomacy, the statements that have been made in the Security Council are quite clear that this is the plan, this is the way we are moving forward. So, while we are not taking an active role, if you ask the actors with whom we may have challenging relationships, they certainly see our role as present.

Ms. ROS-LEHTINEN. Thank you. That is comforting. Thank you. Dr. Wehrey?

Mr. WEHREY. Thank you, Congresswoman.

I think Haftar's removal in the East would just underscore what we have always known, that his coalition was just a coalition. Ever since he launched his operation in May or the summer of 2014, tribes, different religious groups and different militias attached themselves to his operation for their own self-serving purposes. Once he could claim liberation of Benghazi, that coalition has started to unravel. So, even before his health problems, there was also a lot of dissent when I was there in Benghazi, against his style of rule, against the empowerment of his sons, against his political ambitions, his corruption. So, all of this was building. You have different centers of power in the East, three different cities. You have different tribes that are maneuvering.

The bottom line is I think you are going to see jockeying. It may devolve into some violence. I think it is also an opportunity in the sense that, if some new figure emerges at the head of the LNA, the Libyan National Army, that could be more amenable to western Libya, that could be an opportunity for reconciliation. It is important to underscore in western Libya just how demonized Haftar was because of his baggage, because of his political ambitions.

I think the United States has an important role to play with the regional Arab states that backed Haftar, the United Arab Emirates and Egypt. They had already been cooling about General Haftar a bit. He was not delivering for them. I think this just underscores the point that, if these regional states want influence in the new Libya, they need to support the backing of a new figure in the East that is more amenable to reconciliation and unifying the country.

Ms. ROS-LEHTINEN. Thank you so much, Dr. Wehrey.

Ms. Friend?

Ms. FRIEND. Ma'am, I agree with what my colleagues have said. I think there will be a real fight for control of the LNA if he doesn't return. I think who takes over will really matter because, if it is a contentious figure, then the infighting will continue, and if it is a powerful figure——

Ms. ROS-LEHTINEN. Let me just interrupt. When you say "fight for control," will that be a bloody fight for control, an electoral fight for control?

Ms. FRIEND. I think it will be bloody, ma'am. I think, as you pointed out in your comments, we are already perhaps starting to see some of the struggles in today's car bomb attack.

And so, I think there will be several consequences to this that are possible. There could be reduced pressure on violent Islamist groups in the area. Governance of Benghazi will certainly be very different going forward. I think it will interrupt reconciliation between the east and the west, simply because it is unclear who westerners now negotiate with. But it may help continuance of the LPA, which Haftar had announced in December was now defunct. So, I also agree it might be an opportunity. I also think it is going to interrupt Russian influence, at least for a time. They are going to have to figure out where they are going to put their investments now.

On the U.S. side, I tend to focus on the counterterrorism piece. I think it is important the U.S. continue to be extremely discriminating in targeting, because, again, as all of these groups are realigning on the ground, we need to know exactly who we are watching and who the enemies are, and who is simply caught up in a fight, as it were.

When it comes to trafficking, I would just say there is great variance among groups across the Sahel in how much they benefit from and are involved in trafficking, but it does allow them to blend in, if you will. And they are part of a larger illicit criminal network and lawlessness problem. And so, again, from a targeting perspective and figuring out who it is that we are most interested in from an American national security perspective, that just complicates matters.

Ms. ROS-LEHTINEN. Very difficult to figure that out.

Thank you so much.

And I am pleased to yield to Mr. Cicilline.

Mr. CICILLINE. Thank you, Chairman.

Thank you to our witnesses.

The U.N.-appointed Envoy to Libya, Ghassan Salame, plans to amend the 2015 political agreement establishing the current government, hold a national conference, call a referendum on the constitution, and hold elections this year, as I am sure that you are aware and, Dr. Wehrey, you mentioned this. Human Rights Watch warned last month that Libya is not ready to hold free and fair elections, setting concerns about potential coercion, discrimination, and intimidation.

So, I would like to know from each of you, what milestones does Libya need to reach to demonstrate that it is ready, actually, for fair elections? And I suppose, what can the U.S. do to help create the conditions for them to achieve those milestones?

Mr. BLANCHARD. So, to begin, the Libyan electoral authorities have conducted a new voter registration drive, and that is one of the sort of highlights that SRSG Salame points to, that 2.5 million Libyans stepped forward to participate. That shows a baseline of a desire to participate in an election.

The laws surrounding a referendum, the setting of districts, the balance, all that needs to be agreed, and hasn't been. Again, as the Special Representative points out, I think he said at the meeting in Saudi Arabia, some of our Libyan brothers are very creative in their means of preventing action on those electoral issues, the nuts and bolts, right, the electoral structure. That needs to be taking place. So, I would watch that quite carefully.

We saw participation decline over the past electoral exercises. And so, to the extent that we see turnout, that is something to watch very closely. Because, really, what this is about is the legitimacy, the lack of legitimacy in domestic institutions. That is what needs to be reset here.

Mr. CICILLINE. Thank you.

Mr. WEHREY. I think there are a number of key danger points. The first one is the lack of a constitutional framework. I mean, my discussions with Libyans is, without a constitution, whatever government is produced is going to be yet another transitional government that is going to lack legitimacy, lack real authority.

The other key milestones are voting laws, security. My visits to especially eastern Libyan underscored a degree of disenchantment with democracy, that we tried these elections before. Some people want a strongman, and that is why Khalifa Haftar was able to step into the void. And so, people saw that after the 2012, and especially the 2014, voting, there were parliaments that could not deliver to their constituents that were locked in committee disputes, and that led to strife. So, overcoming that popular aversion to elections is important.

Mr. CICILLINE. Thank you.

Anything that you have?

Ms. FRIEND. Yes, sir. I would say that I think a study of the conditions prior to the 2014 elections would be very useful because, of course, those elections were what, then, led to greater disillusion politically inside the country.

And then, just from my own narrow purview, I always say capacity for electoral security is extremely important because elections marred by violence, as we have seen in Kenya and elsewhere, have very poor outcomes as well.

Mr. CICILLINE. Thank you.

Some have argued that, based on the highly fractured nature of Libyan politics, governance may be better suited for a federalized system, granting relative autonomy for various regions. I am wondering whether you believe some manner of federalized Libya might bring about increased security and popular confidence in governance compared to a strong centralized government, where they have had so much, I think, disappointment with that model. Is that a feasible thing to consider?

Mr. BLANCHARD. Decentralization has been a core theme of the political conversation in Libya since 2011. As Fred mentioned, municipalities have stepped forward and into the void to a certain extent. While a Federal arrangement or a decentralized political arrangement may emerge, difficult questions about state resources, the distribution of funding, management of security, all those would remain to be decided and dealt with. And it is likely that those will remain difficult.

Mr. CICILLINE. If I could just have one final question, with the chairman's indulgence? We have heard a lot about outside actors in Libya, and I want to focus for a moment on Russia, which appears to be playing several sides in this conflict. There are claims that Russia has facilitated the delivery of weapons to Haftar's forces, sometimes through legal sales to Egypt, and the Russian special forces are reported to be operating in the porous border region between Egypt and Libya. So, if you could give me your assessment of what is Russia's goal with respect to Libya and what does it have to gain in Libya? And what does the U.S. risk by Russia increasing its influence, or attempting to increase its influence, in the various warring Libyan groups long term?

Mr. WEHREY. I think Russia wants to undercut European and U.S. influence. I think this is an opportunity for them. I think they have a number of financial goals in mind regarding arms contracts, many of which they had before the revolution. Gas deals, they had infrastructure projects. So, I think partly it is monetary, but it is also a political opportunity. I don't think they have got all their eggs in the Haftar basket. I think they are diversifying their contacts to include Misurata, to include Tripoli. They see themselves as a potential power broker. They could certainly undercut the U.S. and the Europeans.

Ms. FRIEND. Yes, sir, I would agree with that. I think they are playing as many sides as possible, so that they will have influence in the eventual government that wins out.

Mr. BLANCHARD. Yes, I mentioned the Security Council earlier. The Russians have the same quiet role that we have and the ability to delay and obstruct.

Mr. CICILLINE. Thank you so much. Thank you, Madam Chairman, and I yield back.

Ms. ROS-LEHTINEN. Thank you, Mr. Cicilline. Excellent questions and great answers.

And now, I am pleased to yield to one of our favorite veterans on our subcommittee——

Mr. KINZINGER. Well, thanks.

Ms. ROS-LEHTINEN [continuing]. Mr. Kinzinger.

Mr. KINZINGER. Thank you. That is very nice. Thank you, Madam Chair.

As I said in the opening, thank you all for being here.

I actually think Libya is an interesting study. With all the challenges we have, it actually could end up, if we figure out how to handle it—it is a very wealthy country with a relatively small population. I also used Libya as kind of the example when people argued, although the situation on the ground has changed a little bit much now, against intervention in Syria. I said, well, you have ½ million dead Syrians. You don't have that level of instability in Libya, even though there is a major challenge.

The problem with Libya is our failure to follow through, I think, what was rightfully an intervention. And then, we just kind of assumed it would all work itself out, and it didn't.

So, I think leaving Libya with no strategy, if we are dealing with a post-Qaddafi world, we can look back in 2020 and say, here is everything. I think it is important for us to talk about, though, what we could have done differently post-Libya, because it would be naive of us to think we will never be in this kind of situation again.

So, Mr. Blanchard, if you have ideas of what we could have done differently? Or else we will go down the panel. I am curious of what you guys would say. If you could go back in time, what would you have changed in order to try to create a better post-Qaddafi scenario?

Mr. BLANCHARD. I think perhaps Alice might be better suited to talk about the Obama administration's view and what the conversation may have been. The President himself has been clear in terms of what he saw as the failure, and it really was, as you mentioned, the assumption not just that it would work itself out, but that the European partners and Arab states would step forward in a coordinated manner.

If we look at the diplomatic level, it really is what SRSG Salame calls too many cooks in the kitchen, and too many cooks maybe with bad intent or their own selfish intent. So, it is that coordinating function, the speaking with one voice, and making sure that there wasn't daylight such that those individual interests could begin to play themselves out and amplify the internal dilemma. So, early coordinated action may have been something that I would focus on.

Mr. KINZINGER. Ms. Friend, actually, if you want to jump into that? And then, we will go to you, sir.

Ms. FRIEND. Yes, sir. By the time I stepped into my Pentagon job in the Africa office, from a DoD perspective, we were already quite cautious because the empowerment of militias, of course, was off and running. And so, it was very hard to know from a security assistance perspective which party not only was aligned with a legitimate government we recognized at the time, but also would continue to be aligned and would continue to be a good-faith actor, which was something that AFRICOM certainly emphasized as well.

Mr. KINZINGER. Did you guys discuss peacekeepers at all, and was that even a possibility?

Ms. FRIEND. I don't recall us discussing peacekeepers at that point. I know that it has been in the ether, especially among some Europeans, for quite a long time. Peacekeeping itself has its own sort of difficult track record as well. Peacekeeping is an extraordinarily difficult thing to do, and it really depends on the parties on the ground wanting to have a peace to keep. And I don't think we were there with Libya yet.

And so, I think the complexity and difficulty of the environment was something that we simply did not recognize long enough into it. And by the time we did, it was very hard to be able to have meaningful influence on the ground, particularly given the security situation for our own personnel.

So, I do wish, if I could rewind the clock, I wish that the U.S. had perhaps taken a more forceful role at the United Nations, that we had been more involved among the parties, although I know Ambassador Stevens could not have been a better person to be there and working that issue.

So, it is possible that Libya is a case where forces on the ground were such that it would have been very, very hard for the United States to do anything unilaterally, but I do think the international community could have put in much more focus and effort in the early days between 2011 and 2012 to perhaps head off the worst of the violence and get the negotiations started sooner.

Mr. KINZINGER. Thank you.

Sir?

Mr. WEHREY. I think in the first year there was an excessive focus on elections as a success marker. And so, the U.N. was entirely focused on elections, to the detriment of dealing with the DDR problem, with the militias, with the security sector. I think the U.S. handed this off to the Europeans and the United Nations, who were both unable and unwilling to address it.

So, you had these elections, but, then, you had no way to protect the democratic institutions from the power of militias. That raises the question of a stabilization force, which I agree brings a whole host of other consequences, but perhaps even a limited stabilization force to secure key facilities in Tripoli, the parliaments, economic institutions, to protect them from militia pressure.

But the huge challenge of demobilizing the militias was made worse when the Libyan Government itself started paying the militias with oil wealth in late 2011. That was a disastrous decision. So, perhaps more U.S. oversight of Libya's use of its oil wealth could have stopped this disaster. I think by the time we got around to trying to train and equip a Libyan military force, the General Purpose Force, it was too late. That effort led to disaster because the militias were too strong. So, again, the bottom line is I think we missed a key window in that first year to exert more of a presence.

Mr. KINZINGER. And I think it is somewhat to the extent of the mistake made in Iraq, where we went in and there was a sense of lawlessness after the invasion instead of law, and people turned.

And, Madam Chair, if I could ask just one more question with leniency?

Ms. ROS-LEHTINEN. Absolutely. Go ahead.

Mr. KINZINGER. We talk about Haftar. Whoever has the knowledge on it—maybe all three of you—how would you compare him and how you would see a Libya under the rule of Haftar, if you will, versus like Qaddafi? Is he more benevolent? Is he as ruthless? I mean, what is kind of the sense there? And I am sure there is no way to really know, but what are your thoughts?

Mr. BLANCHARD. Muammar al-Qaddafi was a very unique individual. So, I would be reticent to compare or expect anyone to equate quite that way.

The fact of the matter is that, personality aside, Libya has changed. The political and security power has been atomized, and any individual and/or ruling arrangement that emerges from this process is going to have to recognize that. In an odd sense, the Libya of Qaddafi's imagination, with individual communities leading themselves and feeding upward. That is, ironically, now more the case than it was when he was there. And so, whoever is leading Libya in the future is going to have to deal with, as I said, this atomization that has occurred.

Mr. KINZINGER. Fair point.

Mr. WEHREY. I think Haftar's support was already weakened. So, he didn't have the sort of total control that Qaddafi had. But, that said, there were a number of similarities that his opponents have drawn and that I witnessed when I was in Benghazi. I mean, he was cultivating his sons. He did sort of enact a cult of personality where you would go around Benghazi and see billboards of Haftar's picture everywhere. The police state, people were not free to speak their minds in Benghazi. People who criticized them disappeared. Censorship of the press. He brought back the old police, secret police. He relies on tribes. He tries to manage tribes, play them off against each other. So, there are some similarities. That said, as we have seen with his failing health and his diminishing influence, I don't think it compares to Qaddafi.

Mr. KINZINGER. Did you have anything else?

Ms. FRIEND. No.

Mr. KINZINGER. Okay. Well, thank you, Madam Chair, and I yield back.

Thank you all.

Ms. ROS-LEHTINEN. Thank you very much, Mr. Kinzinger.

Mr. Connolly of Virginia?

Mr. CONNOLLY. Thank you, Madam Chairman.

And welcome to our panel.

Dr. Wehrey, let me start with you. You said one of the bright spots potentially, not to overstate it, but were kind of at the local level in terms of elections, function. And that was music to my ears. I come from local government. I think it is long neglected. I think a lot of our democracy promotion programs start at the top and we start with the Parliament, as opposed to starting at the village level and working the way up.

Can we build on that, do you think? Could that maybe affect our strategy moving forward, maybe a different course for us in terms of what we pursue in Libya, given the fact there is a hopeful sign, but it is working at the local level?

Mr. WEHREY. Absolutely. I mean, we have seen a number of positive developments where there has been reconciliation between towns that were previously fighting. Towns enjoy strong legitimacy with their elected councils. This was true in 2012 through to the present, although I will caveat this that in the east there are non-elected mayors that have been appointed by the army.

So, American engagement through USAID and through other channels, is absolutely the right way to go; however, not necessarily these non-elected councils. But I think, I mean, helping them to deliver services, the problem, though, also, it goes back to the national level, where they don't get their budgets. They are criticizing the Government of National Accord for the way it distributes its budget. So, I think American engagement has to be from both levels. I mean, the local is important, but it can only get you so far. There has to be engagement at the national level.

Mr. CONNOLLY. Yes, but the thing about local government that all over the world some institutions just don't get it, but if you want to build democracy, it is built on a social contract.

Mr. WEHREY. Absolutely.

Mr. CONNOLLY. I pay my taxes, and you pick up my trash. I pay my taxes; the clinic is open when I need it. I pay my taxes; the road gets paved. I pay my taxes; there is a clean source of water.

If, on the other hand, there is no respect for that and there is no culture of, well, what do you mean we are supposed to make all that work, we don't do that, it is corrupt, not our business, well, then you are going to completely erode confidence in the basic institution of governance, and it is why it exists, let alone democracy and what kind of government. And I think often that gets overlooked. That is why I picked up on what you said as one maybe helpful sign that we could build upon, expand; God forbid we invest in it.

Mr. Blanchard, we have met before and we had a talk about terrorism in the Maghreb. And one of the things I recall you and I talking about, and I want to give you an opportunity to talk about it on the record here, but Libya is kind of key. I mean, if we are going to get at terrorists, well, instability in parts of Tunisia, parts of Nigeria, parts of Morocco, you cannot ignore the big, huge, festering sore of Libya. It is kind of key to addressing all the other potential hotspots in the region.

Could you elaborate a little bit on that and how what we are talking about relates to other things we also care about in the region?

Mr. BLANCHARD. Sure. As I said earlier, I think the United States is one actor among many outside Libya that is seeking to mitigate transnational threats, terrorism in particular. I think terrorism is the key driver of Egypt's desire to back "the strongman approach" to security in eastern Libya.

I think the continued availability of weapons, the ability, particularly on the southern and southwest borders, of people to transit back and forth allows a place for the ISIS fighters that Fred talked about being displaced from Sirte to hide, regroup, to reorganize. I also think that, in terms of our investment, the Department of Defense is, to the extent that we are investing in a sort of long-range counterterrorism approach, it is a containment strategy, and it is built entirely on this. So, it is a draw on our resources as well.

With regard to local communities, I did just want to observe the USAID programs, the Transition Initiatives Programs have a lot of components that are focused precisely on aspects that you raised, you know, helping local communities and local government improve services, take the temperature of the town and see what they need. So, that kind of grassroots approach is one component of our policy. But, as Fred observed, in the absence of a nationwide national political accord, it is going to be difficult for those to really prosper.

Mr. CONNOLLY. Yes, it is harder, and I am a big supporter of both NDI and IRI, and I think they are necessary. But I think sometimes it is easier to work with parliamentarians in the national capital than it is to roll up your sleeves and go down to the village level and try to help them do their jobs, and do it in a way that incorporates accountability and transparency, which are elements of democratic institution-building.

From my own personal experience of working on some projects before I had this job, sometimes we do it well; sometimes we don't. I believe the building block of democracy starts at the local level, not the other way around.

Can I just ask one last question? This is the big philosophical one. But I was in Libya a few years ago with our former colleague, David Dreier, under the House Democracy Project. What struck me about Libya was, unlike some other places, you essentially have three population centers. They are all near the coast. You don't have a huge interior population. It is, relative to some other places, not all that heterogeneous; it is a pretty homogeneous population. Tribal divisions, yes, but they used to, I mean, they are just coming off one-man rule for quite a long time. You could call that stability, not one we desire, but it is not like it is a novel thought that there could be a government, a central government, that exercises authority. It is a small population.

So, why is this so hard? Why has it already been so long that we see this kind of chaos, this inability to put together meaningful coalitions that can govern and into which the population can invest and support? Why is it so hard?

Mr. WEHREY. Congressman, thank you.

I agree. I mean, these were all things that led to our optimism after the 2011 revolution. I think the fundamental problem is Qaddafi ruined this country. He gutted it of institutions. So, Libyans had no experience in self-governance. The entire muscle fiber you need to run a country was missing. Qaddafi ruled this in a highly personalized way.

So, things like civil society, unions, elected municipal councils, they were all starting from scratch. And the fundamental vacuum is also the security sector. I mean, there was no army. So, you had the growth of these militias. You had, unfortunately, during the revolution and after, you did have real divisions growing between these different towns that acted like autonomous statelets that coalesced with their own militias, their own sources of income.

I agree it is a small population; it should be easier. But the final thing I will add is the management of the economy. As the U.N. has mentioned, at its core, this is a contest for plunder, for access to economic resources. So, the economy is both, I think, a blessing and a curse.

Ms. FRIEND. Sir, can I just say, historically thinking, the idea of Libya as one unified country is actually an anomaly. It is a very regional organization. In fact, there was no, there still is no rail line between eastern and western. It is very hard to drive. There is just not a lot of infrastructure integration between east and west. And the Fezzan in the south has always been isolated.

And so, I think, at least from a regional perspective, even though it is a small population, there actually isn't a tradition of integration across regions in Libya. And so, to some extent, this is a project that is imposing a new concept on Libya, Qaddafi notwithstanding. I mean, I think he papered over a lot of things and just did it through strength of arms.

And I was intrigued by what Mr. Blanchard had said about how the hangover from Qaddafi is such that there is now a deep suspicion of centralized authority. So, it is not a historical tradition, and with Qaddafi as their example, why should the average person in Benghazi or Derna trust the Tripoli government? And this is what folks there have to overcome.

Mr. CONNOLLY. Thank you.

Mr. BLANCHARD. I wouldn't want to let the international community off the hook. As I said, seeking to mitigate transitional threats or pursuing their own agendas, political, regional, ideological, has led to a lot of interference, and it has amplified the real internal challenges and difficult dilemmas, zero-sum behavior, security threats, that Libyans are facing. When you have outsiders coming in, observing a difficult situation, and saying, well, "I need to back this person to solve my problem," that has an amplifying effect, and it has really, I think, helped account for what we have seen subsequently.

Mr. CONNOLLY. Madam Chairman, you have been so gracious, but it has been a very thoughtful conversation.

Ms. ROS-LEHTINEN. Thank you very much.

Mr. CONNOLLY. And thank you.

Ms. ROS-LEHTINEN. I pay my taxes, and I want clean water. I pay my taxes. I got it.

Thank you so much, Mr. Connolly.

I would like to ask, if you would allow me, the questions that Mr. Deutch had. And they have kind of been covered a little bit, but I want to make sure that his are covered extensively.

First, "The U.N. Refugee Agency estimates that there are 1.1 million people in Libya in need of humanitarian assistance. Displaced families, refugees, and those living without basic services or health care continue to demonstrate Libya's need for assistance."

So, Mr. Deutch asks, "Do you think the U.S. is providing adequate levels of humanitarian assistance to Libya, and what gaps remain where the U.S. or our international partners could step up?"

Mr. Blanchard?

Mr. BLANCHARD. I am looking for the data points that I brought with me because I want to get this right.

So, there is an International Humanitarian Response Plan for Libya. The United States is the top contributor in 2016 and 2017 of humanitarian funding by just a hair. The Germans and the Italians, the Europeans also put forward funds to support that.

The needs that have been identified I think were 70 percent met last year. Could more be done, particularly with regard to the migrant situation? The United States approach has been, I think, to let European states and the European Union take the lead there. Working together, the European Union, the African Union, and the U.N. have taken some steps to address that problem. Again, the United States, I think, declaratory policy is quite supportive of that, and behind the scenes we are making a contribution.

Mr. WEHREY. Chairman, I would defer to Mr. Blanchard on the actual specifics, but let me just underscore that the refugee displacement issue is so profound, and I saw it firsthand. I mean hundreds of families displaced from the city of Benghazi are crowded into other cities in the west, Misrata and Tripoli. There are refugees from the south that are in the capital. So, these refugees are straining the ability of the government in the capital.

You have other local communities that have been displaced through fighting. The city of Tawergha is the main example, and I have been in their camps. There are truly horrific conditions, you know, young kids growing up year after year in these squalid refugee camps. So, it is a huge moral problem.

The U.S. I think can always be doing more. I think its role, however, should be focused on Libyan economic institutions that can better address the plight of those displaced economically. So, there again, that leads me back to U.S. engagement with the Central Bank.

Ms. ROS-LEHTINEN. Thank you.

Ms. Friend?

Ms. FRIEND. Madam Chairman, Ranking Member Deutch mentioned root causes. I think in this case it is important to distinguish between the humanitarian needs from the Libyan population as a result of the violence and, then, the humanitarian needs of the migrant population coming from sub-Saharan African largely.

And when it comes to humanitarian needs for the Libyans, to address that, of course, involves addressing the root causes of the violence. And so, that, again, gets us back to these reconciliation efforts.

And when it comes to the sub-Saharan Africans, then that is also its own set of root humanitarian and governance issues that are driving people out of their homes. So, we think of about Eritreans crossing the desert in Sudan to get to Libya, to get across the Mediterranean. Addressing what is happening in Eritrea or what is happening in Niger, or Mali, I think is as important as catching the problem by the time it gets to Libya.

Ms. ROS-LEHTINEN. Thank you very much.

And his second question—thank you for those answers—"The U.S. and the U.N. continue striving to work through the existing framework established under the Libyan Political Agreement to establish and move Libya forward. Some, however, do not recognize this agreement's legitimacy. In your opinion, do you believe this framework is viable or does a new path need to be forged?"

Mr. BLANCHARD. I think the SRSG's current approach is driven by, as I said in my opening statement, a desire to refresh the legitimacy of institutions, in particular, so that decisions can be taken by a recognized authority. So, in terms of a legitimacy deficit, it is clear—not necessarily that we in the United States get to decide that or point to it; it is the Libyans themselves who think that various institutions lack legitimacy. And so, this entire exercise is, arguably, aimed at that.

Mr. WEHREY. I agree. I mean, I think this was an important starting point. It was flawed. Certainly, it was opposed. But it was at least a mark on the wall. And so, before you peer into the abyss and jump into it, you have to have something to replace it. So, I think the U.N.'s approach with amendments, with reviving it, giving it new legitimacy, is the right approach. Of course, there are multiple actors across the board that benefit from the status quo, and spoiling it. Some of these actors are backed by international states. And that is why I think the U.S. has an important convening role to get everyone on the same page to say, let's move forward on this roadmap. This LPA certainly was flawed, but was signed up to, and it needs to be the basis.

Ms. FRIEND. Ma'am, I addressed in my written testimony the security elements of the LPA, which I think in principle are very good. The problem with the implementation has been making the leap, as I say, from militias to a national military force.

In particular for the HOR and Tobruk that works with Haftar, the issue has been command and control and the Presidential Council being the Commander-in-Chief of the armed forces with which elements of the HOR are not comfortable.

So, I think in these discussions, if these issues can be worked out, the framework of the LPA from a security perspective is quite sound.

Ms. Ros-Lehtinen. Well, we alternate between high hopes, low expectations, and it is just some kind of wild ride. And unfortunately, so many lives are at stake.

Thank you so much for excellent testimony.

And please tell Mr. Deutch that I did comply with his questions. I did my homework.

Excellent witnesses. Thank you.

With that, the subcommittee is adjourned.

[Whereupon, at 3:15 p.m., the subcommittee was adjourned.]

APPENDIX

Material Submitted for the Record

SUBCOMMITTEE HEARING NOTICE
COMMITTEE ON FOREIGN AFFAIRS
U.S. HOUSE OF REPRESENTATIVES
WASHINGTON, DC 20515-6128

Subcommittee on the Middle East and North Africa
Ileana Ros-Lehtinen (R-FL), Chairman

April 11, 2018

TO: MEMBERS OF THE COMMITTEE ON FOREIGN AFFAIRS

You are respectfully requested to attend an OPEN hearing of the Committee on Foreign Affairs to be held by the Subcommittee on the Middle East and North Africa in Room 2172 of the Rayburn House Office Building (and available live on the Committee website at http://www.ForeignAffairs.house.gov).

DATE: Wednesday, April 18, 2018

TIME: 2:00 p.m.

SUBJECT: Libya Fractured: The Struggle for Unity

WITNESSES: Mr. Christopher Blanchard
Specialist in Middle Eastern Affairs
Congressional Research Institute

Frederic Wehrey, Ph. D.
Senior Fellow for Middle East Program
Carnegie Endowment for International Peace

Ms. Alice Hunt Friend
Senior Fellow for International Security Program
Center for Strategic and International Studies

By Direction of the Chairman

COMMITTEE ON FOREIGN AFFAIRS

MINUTES OF SUBCOMMITTEE ON _________ *Middle East and North Africa* _________ HEARING

Day __*Wednesday*__ Date_____ *04.18.18* _____ Room_____ *2172* _____

Starting Time ___ *2:06 p.m.* ___ Ending Time ___ *3:15 p.m* ___

Recesses |___| (___to___) (___to___) (___to___) (___to___) (___to___) (___to___)

Presiding Member(s)

Chairman Ros-Lehtinen

Check all of the following that apply:

Open Session ☑   Electronicall   y Recorded (taped) ☑
Executive (closed) Session ☐   Stenographic Record ☑
Televised ☑

TITLE OF HEARING:

Libya Fractured: The Struggle for Unity

SUBCOMMITTEE MEMBERS PRESENT:

GOP: Reps. Chabot, DeSantis, Kinzinger, Zeldin
Dem: Ranking Member Deutch, Reps. Connolly, Cicilline, Schneider

NON-SUBCOMMITTEE MEMBERS PRESENT: *(Mark with an * if they are not members of full committee.)*

HEARING WITNESSES: Same as meeting notice attached? Yes ☑ No ☐
(If "no", please list below and include title, agency, department, or organization.)

STATEMENTS FOR THE RECORD: *(List any statements submitted for the record.)*

Statement for the Record Submitted by Rep. Connolly

TIME SCHEDULED TO RECONVENE _________
or
TIME ADJOURNED ___ *3:15 p.m.* ___

Subcommittee Staff Associate

Statement for the Record
Submitted by Mr. Connolly of Virginia

More than two years after the December 2015 agreement to establish a Government of National Accord in Libya, rival political factions continue to obstruct the creation of a cohesive national government. Libya's security has dissolved into a puzzle of sub-state actors, militias, and violent extremist groups. With no national government and warring tribal rivalries running rampant around the country, Libya is a growing exporter of terrorism that is threatening its neighbors and undermining U.S. national security interests. The Trump Administration must understand that Libya is key to achieving broader U.S. counterterrorism objectives in the Middle East North Africa region.

Separate governing entities in eastern and western Libya have impeded the Government of National Accord's (GNA) progress. The western Libya-based GNA leaders have begun to administer some government agencies, but have not consolidated national control. The eastern Libya-based House of Representatives (HOR), and a group of military officers aligned with the Libyan National Army (LNA) led by retired General Khalifa Haftar, operate a parallel government that challenges the GNA's legitimacy. In late 2017, the United Nations launched the "Action Plan for Libya," which aims to complete Libya's political transition this year, but ongoing disputes threaten the plan's success.

The United States and our European partners recognize the GNA as Libya's best hope for peace and stability, and have supported its development accordingly. However, not all governing entities in Libya have signed onto the GNA, and questions remain over unified political leadership and military command, national finances, and control of oil infrastructure. International backing for the GNA has led some Libyan contingents to describe GNA leaders as "foreign-imposed interlopers." HOR members aligned with General Haftar take specific issue with recognizing the GNA Presidency Council as the legitimate leaders of Libya's armed forces.

Libya's weak governance has allowed numerous armed groups to occupy territory throughout the country. Thanks in part to U.S. military support, the Libyan branch of ISIL has largely been defeated, but other radical jihadist and secular militia groups continue to battle for regional control. According to Tunisia's Ambassador to the U.S., at least four terrorist attacks in Tunisia between March 2015 and March 2016 were planned from Libya. We cannot have a major failed state at the nexus of this region exporting violence to neighboring vulnerable countries. This ongoing conflict has opened up the country to a host of problems, including human trafficking; illegal migration; institutional rivalries; as well as food, fuel, and power shortages.

Recent reports have detailed disturbing conditions for migrants and refugees in forced labor and slave auctions by both state and non-state actors. The House Foreign Affairs Committee recently passed H. Res. 644, which I was glad to cosponsor. The resolution condemns the exploitation of these migrants and refugees in Libya, and calls on the Government of Libya, the United Nations, and the African Union to investigate the existence of slave auctions in Libya and hold those involved accountable. It also calls on the State Department and USAID to use appropriated funds for humanitarian assistance for migrants and refugees in detention centers and to develop a holistic strategy for Libya.

I hope our witnesses will illuminate how the United States, in conjunction with our international and Libyan partners, can support compromise and demilitarization among Libya's rival factions and root out transnational terrorist threats. Ensuring a peaceful resolution and democratic governance will be an essential foundation to begin to address the many obstacles impeding Libya's progress. The road ahead is treacherous, but it is critical that the United States remain engaged to help Libya form a stable and united national government, and to support U.S. counterterrorism efforts across the region.